Your
Checking
Account

Lessons in Personal Banking

STUDENT BOOK

REVISED EDITION

by Victoria W. Reitz

WALCH PUBLISHING

1   3   4   5   6   7   8   9   10

ISBN 0-8251-5912-1

Copyright © 1987, 1993, 2000, 2006
J. Weston Walch, Publisher
P.O. Box 658 • Portland, Maine 04104-0658
www.walch.com

Printed in the United States of America

Distributed By:
Grass Roots Press
Toll Free: 1-888-303-3213
Fax: (780) 413-6582
Web Site: www.grassrootsbooks.net

⌘ Contents

Introduction ....*v*

Part 1: Understanding Your Checking Account

Opening a Checking Account 3

Applying for and Using an Automated Teller Machine Card and/or Debit Card ... 5

Checking Deposit Slips 8

ATM Deposit 13

Checks 13

Check Register 15

Endorsing Checks 19

Bank Costs 21

Finding the Best Bank 22

Lost Checks or ATM/Debit Cards 23

Reconciling Your Checking Account 23

Making Your Records Agree 31

Keeping Track of Expenses 31

Part 2: Six-Month Banking Simulation

Introduction 37

January 37

February 54

March 62

April 71

May 79

June 88

Deposit Record 96

Deposit Slips 97

Check Register Pages 107

Blank Checks 113

⌘ Introduction

One day you will reach the age at which most of your mail is bills. You could go to each business and pay cash, but there is an easier way. A checking account will let you pay by mail.

To have a checking account, you must first put money in an account at a bank. You will need to buy checks to use as cash. When you write a check, you are ordering the bank to pay a certain amount of money to that individual or business. Certain businesses will allow you to use an automated teller machine card. This is a special card provided by the bank. It lets you transfer money from your account to the business you are buying from.

Here are some good reasons to have a checking account:

❐ Cash can be stolen.

❐ If you lose a check, the bank can stop it from being cashed.

❐ You won't have to carry a large amount of cash with you.

❐ It is easier and quicker to pay bills.

❐ A check is a record of a bill that you have paid. If you need to prove you paid for something, you can get a copy of the check from the bank for a small fee.

❐ An automated teller machine card will also allow you to get cash, make deposits, transfer money between accounts, check your balances, and make most of your regular transactions.

❐ A debit card will allow you to do everything an automated teller card allows you to do and also allows you to access funds from your checking account wherever you see a major credit symbol that matches your debit card.

In this book, you will learn how to open a checking account and how to keep track of the money in your account. The first part of this book, Understanding Your Checking Account, will tell you how a checking account works. The second part, Six-Month Banking Simulation, will give you practice managing a checking account.

Part 1: Understanding Your Checking Account

⌘ Opening a Checking Account

There are several types of checking accounts. The two most common are:

❐ **Draft (Checking) Account**—No minimum balance is required. You will have a monthly service charge or per check charge. Overdraft protection out of an adjoining savings is available. This account can be for a single individual or multiple people.

❐ **Preferred Draft (Checking) Account**—A checking account with no minimum balance requirement or per check charges. You receive unlimited free checks, death insurance, and many other benefits including vacation and travel benefits—all for a small monthly fee. Free overdraft protection is available. This account can be used for a single individual or multiple people.

You must fill out a form before you can open a checking account. This form shows how you write your name. It is illegal for anyone else to sign your name to a check. This form will help the bank protect you against this. A bank manager or assistant will help you open your checking account. Federal law requires all financial institutions to obtain, verify, and record information that identifies each person who opens an account. Your name, address, date of birth, and other important information that identifies you will be asked for. They may also ask to see your driver's license or other identifying documents. This information helps the government fight against the funding of terrorist and money laundering activities.

Here is an example of this type of form:

Full Name _____

Address _____

City _____ State _____ Zip _____

SSN _____ DOB _____

Driver's Lic # _____

Phone _____

Present Employer _____

Type of Account Desired

        Regular Savings ____
        Draft (Checking) ____
        Preferred Draft (Checking) ____
        Other ____

Do you wish to have anyone joint with you on your account? If yes, fill out the information below.

Full Name _____

Address _____

City _____ State _____ Zip _____

SSN _____ DOB _____

Driver's Lic # _____

Phone _____

Member Signature _____

Joint Owner Signature _____

⌘ Fill in the blank form below. Use your own name and address. When you finish, have your teacher check it.

Full Name _____

Address _____

City _____ State _____ Zip _____

SSN _____ DOB _____

Driver's Lic # _____

Phone _____

Present Employer _____

Type of Account Desired

      Regular Savings ____
      Draft (Checking) ____
      Preferred Draft (Checking) ____
      Other ____

Do you wish to have anyone joint with you on your account? If yes, fill out the information below.

Full Name _____

Address _____

City _____ State _____ Zip _____

SSN _____ DOB _____

Driver's Lic # _____

Phone _____

Member Signature _____

Joint Owner Signature _____

⌘ Applying for and Using an Automated Teller Machine Card and/or Debit Card

An **automated teller machine (ATM) card** can be used to do the following:

❑ Withdraw cash from your checking or savings account

❑ Deposit cash or checks into your checking or savings account

❑ Transfer money between your checking and savings accounts

❑ Check the balances in your savings and checking accounts

❑ Change your personal identification number (PIN) and use it immediately

You can use your card at any network location. The transaction is recorded at your own institution. Some automated teller machines may not be open 24 hours a day, and they may not accept deposits or may limit the deposit you can make.

The following are some features of a debit card:

❑ Can be used just like an ATM card

❑ Lets you use money from your checking account without writing a check

❑ May be accepted by businesses in place of checks

❑ Helps you manage your money better than a regular credit card

❑ Offers you cash advances around the world

❑ Is faster and easier than writing a check

Having either of these cards is safer than carrying a large amount of cash. ATM cards and debit cards are both very convenient because you can still use them when your bank is closed.

If either your card or your PIN becomes lost or stolen, notify your bank. Don't use your cards for another person and don't give them to anyone to use. Remember, do not leave your receipt at the ATM. Take it with you. It is best to keep these receipts so you can check them against your bank statement.

Here is an example of a completed automated teller machine card/debit card application:

(Please Print Carefully)

Chris   V.   Muhlenkamp
First Name   Middle Initial   Last Name

55 Park Avenue   Elka Park,   ME
Street Number   City   State

99999   207-555-5678   207-555-1234
Zip Code   Phone No. (Home)   Phone No. (Work)

123–45–6789   02/08/80
Social Security No.   Date of Birth

MMC CARD NUMBER: **PIN:**

Account Type (Checking, Savings)	Account Number	Account Title (Optional)
Checking	0439628321-4	
Savings	0438149175-6	

I (We) have received the rules and regulations that control the use of the MMC card and agree to the terms that govern its use. It is further agreed that I (we) will follow the rules and regulations of the issuing institution that deals with the accounts indicated.

Applicant(s) signature *Chris Muhlenkamp*   Date 09/10/07

This application is filled out for one person to receive a card. Only Chris Muhlenkamp is allowed to use this account.

Fill in the blank card application below. Use your own name and address. When you finish, have your teacher check it. The bank (teacher) will give you a card number and help you choose a PIN.

(Please Print Carefully)

_____

First Name   Middle Initial   Last Name

_____

Street Number   City   State

_____

Zip Code   Phone No. (Home)   Phone No. (Work)

_____

Social Security No.   Date of Birth

MMC CARD NUMBER: _____ **PIN:** _____

Account Type   Account Number   Account Title
(Checking, Savings)   (Optional)

_____

_____

_____

_____

_____

I (We) have received the rules and regulations that control the use of the MMC card and agree to the terms that govern its use. It is further agreed that I (we) will follow the rules and regulations of the issuing institution that deals with the accounts indicated.

Applicant(s) signature _____ Date _____

⌘ Automated teller machine and debit card

The automated teller machine (ATM) will show you exactly what to do. Just follow the directions that appear on the screen. The basic steps for most machines are:

1. Insert your ATM or debit card.

2. Enter your PIN.

3. Select the transaction (deposit, cash, transfer). The choices will appear on the screen.

4. Use the keyboard to enter the amount of money involved in the transaction.

5. Always follow the instructions on the screen. If you make a mistake, press *no* or *cancel.*

6. You can make as many transactions as you want. When you are finished, the machine will return your card and print a receipt for each transaction. Some machines may not accept deposits or may limit the amount of your deposit. Keep the receipt to record the activity in your check record.

⌘ Checking Deposit Slips

To put money into your checking account, you must first fill out a deposit slip. Your checking account number must be on the depoit slip. The bank will give you deposit slips with your checks, or you can fill out a blank deposit slip at the bank. You must also list the amount of cash and checks that you are depositing. All checks should be listed separately. If you want to get some spending money back, write the amount on the "Less cash received" line. This amount is subtracted from the total. The answer is then placed on the "Net deposit" line.

Remember to add deposits to the last balance recorded in your checkbook. The bank will check the deposit slip. Then you can record the amount in the front of the check register where the deposit record is kept. If you use the automated teller machine, the transaction is automatically reported to the bank. Be sure to record these transactions.

Here is an example of a checking deposit slip.

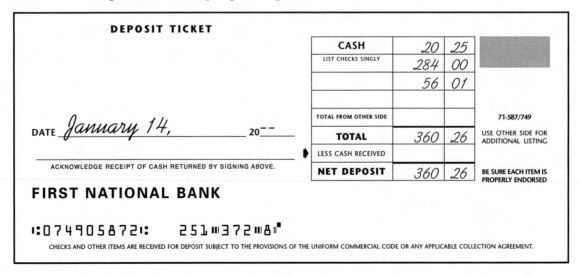

You can see from the deposit slip that the following was deposited: two $10 bills, one quarter, and two checks—$284.00 and $56.01.

Here is another example of a checking deposit slip, but this person wanted some cash back. Look at the "Less cash received" line. $30.00 is the amount that she wants back in cash. Here is what was deposited: three checks—$43.23, $56.78, and $5.65.

DEPOSIT TICKET

CASH		
LIST CHECKS SINGLY	43	23
	56	78
	5	65
TOTAL FROM OTHER SIDE		
TOTAL	105	66
LESS CASH RECEIVED	30	00
NET DEPOSIT	75	66

DATE *February 10,*   20 – –

Jane Doe

ACKNOWLEDGE RECEIPT OF CASH RETURNED BY SIGNING ABOVE

71-587/749

USE OTHER SIDE FOR ADDITIONAL LISTING

BE SURE EACH ITEM IS PROPERLY ENDORSED

FIRST NATIONAL BANK

⑃074905872⑃   251⑈372⑈8⑈"

CHECKS AND OTHER ITEMS ARE RECEIVED FOR DEPOSIT SUBJECT TO THE PROVISIONS OF THE UNIFORM COMMERCIAL CODE OR ANY APPLICABLE COLLECTION AGREEMENT.

⌘ Fill in a practice deposit slip requesting cash. Use the following information to fill in the deposit slip: Use today's date and your name. Deposit this money: two checks—$566.65 and $21.00. Request $45.00 back in cash.

DEPOSIT TICKET

CASH		
LIST CHECKS SINGLY		
TOTAL FROM OTHER SIDE		
TOTAL		
LESS CASH RECEIVED		
NET DEPOSIT		

DATE _____   20_____

_____

ACKNOWLEDGE RECEIPT OF CASH RETURNED BY SIGNING ABOVE

71-587/749

USE OTHER SIDE FOR ADDITIONAL LISTING

BE SURE EACH ITEM IS PROPERLY ENDORSED

FIRST NATIONAL BANK

⑃074905872⑃   251⑈372⑈8⑈"

CHECKS AND OTHER ITEMS ARE RECEIVED FOR DEPOSIT SUBJECT TO THE PROVISIONS OF THE UNIFORM COMMERCIAL CODE OR ANY APPLICABLE COLLECTION AGREEMENT.

Here is another deposit slip example. This time there were more than three checks to list. The customer turned the deposit slip over and listed the extra checks there. After totaling the back, she placed the figure under "Total from other side." She added all the lines up and placed the figure under "Total." This is the amount of all the money in checks and cash. The following was deposited: six checks—$9.82, $126.84, $57.41, $10.22, $11.96, and $187.23.

DEPOSIT TICKET

CASH		
LIST CHECKS SINGLY	9	82
	126	84
	57	41
TOTAL FROM OTHER SIDE	209	41
TOTAL	403	48
LESS CASH RECEIVED		
NET DEPOSIT	403	48

71-587/749

USE OTHER SIDE FOR ADDITIONAL LISTING

BE SURE EACH ITEM IS PROPERLY ENDORSED

DATE *February 10,* 20 – –

ACKNOWLEDGE RECEIPT OF CASH RETURNED BY SIGNING ABOVE.

FIRST NATIONAL BANK

⑈074905872⑈ 251⑆372⑈8⑊

CHECKS AND OTHER ITEMS ARE RECEIVED FOR DEPOSIT SUBJECT TO THE PROVISIONS OF THE UNIFORM COMMERCIAL CODE OR ANY APPLICABLE COLLECTION AGREEMENT.

Back side of deposit ticket:

CHECKS LIST SINGLY	DOLLARS	CENTS																			TOTAL
1	10	22																			209 41
2	11	96																			
3	187	23																			

ENTER TOTAL ON THE FRONT OF THIS TICKET

✤ Fill in the following deposit slip with the information given. Use today's date.
Deposit the following: two quarters, one $50 bill, four checks—$12.50, $120.80,
$360.20, and $127.50.

DEPOSIT TICKET			
	CASH		
	LIST CHECKS SINGLY		
			71-587/749
	TOTAL FROM OTHER SIDE		
DATE _____ 20_____	**TOTAL**		USE OTHER SIDE FOR ADDITIONAL LISTING
➤	LESS CASH RECEIVED		
_____ ACKNOWLEDGE RECEIPT OF CASH RETURNED BY SIGNING ABOVE.	**NET DEPOSIT**		BE SURE EACH ITEM IS PROPERLY ENDORSED

FIRST NATIONAL BANK

⑈074905872⑈   251⑈372⑈8⑈

CHECKS AND OTHER ITEMS ARE RECEIVED FOR DEPOSIT SUBJECT TO THE PROVISIONS OF THE UNIFORM COMMERCIAL CODE OR ANY APPLICABLE COLLECTION AGREEMENT.

CHECKS LIST SINGLY	DOLLARS	CENTS
1		
2		
3		
4		
5		
6		
7		
8		
9		
10		
11		
12		
13		
14		
15		
16		
17		
18		
19		
TOTAL		

ENTER TOTAL ON THE FRONT OF THIS TICKET

⌘ Using all the information given on filling out deposit slips, complete the slip below. Use your name and today's date. Deposit the following: five nickels, six checks—$4.23, $56.23, $345.56, $45.67, $237.99, and $178.44. You also want $165.25 in cash.

DEPOSIT TICKET

CASH		
LIST CHECKS SINGLY		
TOTAL FROM OTHER SIDE		71-587/749
TOTAL		USE OTHER SIDE FOR ADDITIONAL LISTING
LESS CASH RECEIVED		
NET DEPOSIT		BE SURE EACH ITEM IS PROPERLY ENDORSED

DATE _____ 20_____

_____

ACKNOWLEDGE RECEIPT OF CASH RETURNED BY SIGNING ABOVE.

FIRST NATIONAL BANK

⑈074905872⑈ 251⑈372⑈8⑈

CHECKS AND OTHER ITEMS ARE RECEIVED FOR DEPOSIT SUBJECT TO THE PROVISIONS OF THE UNIFORM COMMERCIAL CODE OR ANY APPLICABLE COLLECTION AGREEMENT.

CHECKS LIST SINGLY	DOLLARS	CENTS
1		
2		
3		
4		
5		
6		
7		
8		
9		
10		
11		
12		
13		
14		
15		
16		
17		
18		
19		
TOTAL		

ENTER TOTAL ON THE FRONT OF THIS TICKET

⌘ ATM Deposit

The following is an example of an automated teller machine (ATM) or debit card deposit slip.

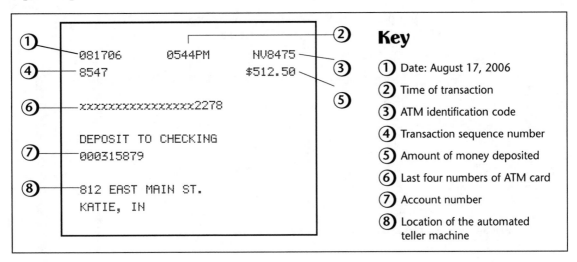

① 081706 0544PM NV8475 ②	**Key**
④ 8547 $512.50 ③	① Date: August 17, 2006
⑤	② Time of transaction
⑥ xxxxxxxxxxxxxxx2278	③ ATM identification code
	④ Transaction sequence number
DEPOSIT TO CHECKING	⑤ Amount of money deposited
⑦ 000315879	⑥ Last four numbers of ATM card
	⑦ Account number
⑧ 812 EAST MAIN ST. KATIE, IN	⑧ Location of the automated teller machine

⌘ Checks

All checks should be written in ink. Why? Because penciled numbers can be erased and changed to a larger amount. And always remember to sign your name and not print it. Below is an example of a check.

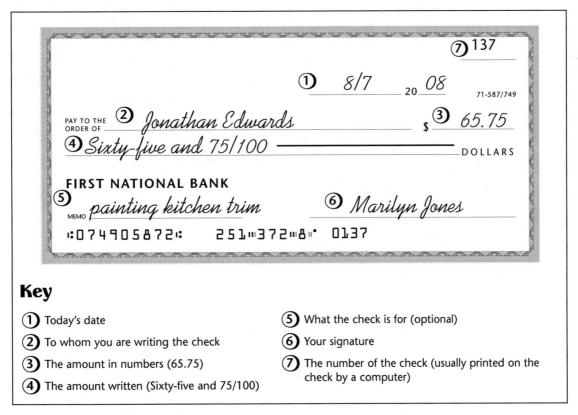

Key

① Today's date

② To whom you are writing the check

③ The amount in numbers (65.75)

④ The amount written (Sixty-five and 75/100)

⑤ What the check is for (optional)

⑥ Your signature

⑦ The number of the check (usually printed on the check by a computer)

⌘ Use the following information to fill out two checks. Follow the example shown to complete them. Be sure to spell everything correctly.

CHECK NO. 90—You buy a pair of boots for $123.50 at Kaye's Shoe Store.
Use your name when signing the check.

_____

_____ 20 _____ 71-587/749

PAY TO THE
ORDER OF _____ $ _____

_____ D O L L A R S

FIRST NATIONAL BANK

MEMO _____   _____

⑆074905872⑆   251⑈372⑈8⑉   0090

CHECK NO. 91—You buy some groceries at Mikshi's Food Store for $19.00.
Use your name when signing the check.

_____

_____ 20 _____ 71-587/749

PAY TO THE
ORDER OF _____ $ _____

_____ D O L L A R S

FIRST NATIONAL BANK

MEMO _____   _____

⑆074905872⑆   251⑈372⑈8⑉   0091

⌘ **Check Register**

When you write a check, you should always keep a record for yourself. A record book, or check register, will come with your checks when you order them from the bank. These record sheets might be separate from the checks or connected to the checks. The following record sheets are in a book separate from the checks. Whether you use your debit card or write a check to pay a bill, you should always record the information immediately. This will keep your records accurate.

Remember, fill out the record sheet first; then write the check or use your debit card. Don't wait until later—you might forget. Here is an example of a filled-in record sheet.

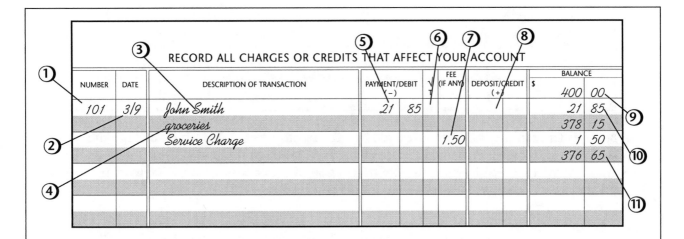

Key

(1) Check number

(2) Date when the check was written

(3) To whom the check was written

(4) What the check was written for

(5) The amount of the check

(6) Make a check mark in this space when the check has been cashed and you receive the statement of your checking account from the bank.

(7) Money charged by the bank for servicing your checking account

(8) The amount of your deposit

(9) The amount of money in your account. The number that you put here is the bottom number from the page before.

(10) The amount of the check that you recorded

(11) The amount of money now in your checking account

If you use an ATM, enter it in your register as you would a check or a deposit. Under "Number" put *ATM,* and under "Description of Transaction" write whether it was a cash withdrawal or a deposit. Then list the amount under the correct heading and add it to or subtract it from the past balance.

If you use your debit card, enter it in your register as you would a check or a deposit. Under "Number" put *debit,* and under "Description of Transaction" write in either the business that you paid, as you would for a check, or the word *deposit.* Then list the amount as you would a check or a deposit.

⌘ Fill in the following record sheet with this information: The starting balance is $149.99. Write check number 227 on 5/4 to Kaye's Paint Shop for two gallons of paint. The cost is $34.26. Remember, checks are subtracted from the last recorded balance. Write in that you used your debit card on 5/6 at Renae's Sail Academy for lessons. The cost was $43.98. This item is also subtracted.

		RECORD ALL CHARGES OR CREDITS THAT AFFECT YOUR ACCOUNT						
NUMBER	DATE	DESCRIPTION OF TRANSACTION	PAYMENT/DEBIT (−)	√ T	FEE (IF ANY)	DEPOSIT/CREDIT (+)	$ BALANCE	

Below is an example of a deposit recorded on the record sheet. A deposit is added to the last balance recorded. The amount deposited was $125.87. Notice under "Description of Transaction" that *deposit* was written. A description of the deposit may also be written in this space (for example, whether it was from a paycheck or a gift).

		RECORD ALL CHARGES OR CREDITS THAT AFFECT YOUR ACCOUNT						
NUMBER	DATE	DESCRIPTION OF TRANSACTION	PAYMENT/DEBIT (−)	√ T	FEE (IF ANY)	DEPOSIT/CREDIT (+)	$ BALANCE	
							93	82
—	3/8	Deposit				125 87	125	87
							219	69

⌘ Fill in the following record sheet with the given information. You deposited $369.00 at the bank on 6/12. Later that evening you also deposited $100.00 using your ATM card. The last recorded balance was $212.36.

		RECORD ALL CHARGES OR CREDITS THAT AFFECT YOUR ACCOUNT						
NUMBER	DATE	DESCRIPTION OF TRANSACTION	PAYMENT/DEBIT (−)	√ T	FEE (IF ANY)	DEPOSIT/CREDIT (+)	$ BALANCE	

⌘ Practice filling out the following checks and record them on the record sheet. A deposit will also need to be recorded. Your beginning balance is $1000.00. Use today's date and your name.

CHECK NO. 100—You paid $321.12 for appliances from Steve's Refrigeration.

	20 ___ 71-587/749
PAY TO THE ORDER OF _____	$ _____
_____ DOLLARS	
FIRST NATIONAL BANK	
MEMO _____	
⑆074905872⑆ 251⑈372⑈8⑈ 00100	

CHECK NO. 101—You bought a shirt from Harmon's. The cost was $22.56.

	20 ___ 71-587/749
PAY TO THE ORDER OF _____	$ _____
_____ DOLLARS	
FIRST NATIONAL BANK	
MEMO _____	
⑆074905872⑆ 251⑈372⑈8⑈ 0101	

Fill in the following record sheet with the information from the checks above. Then list the following deposit. You deposited $562.30. Use today's date. Remember, checks are subtracted and deposits are added.

		RECORD ALL CHARGES OR CREDITS THAT AFFECT YOUR ACCOUNT					
NUMBER	DATE	DESCRIPTION OF TRANSACTION	PAYMENT/DEBIT (−)	√ T	FEE (IF ANY)	DEPOSIT/CREDIT (+)	BALANCE $

⌘ Write the following check and record it on the record sheet. Use today's date and your name. The beginning balance is $369.26. Look at the ATM receipt and debit receipt, and record both on the record sheet.

CHECK NO. 102—You paid $43.23 to Betsy's Moose Shoppe.

```
                                                          20 ____    71-587/749

PAY TO THE
ORDER OF _____   $ _____

_____  DOLLARS

FIRST NATIONAL BANK

MEMO _____    _____

⑈074905872⑈    251⑈372⑈8⑈  0102
```

```
------      0844AM      BE1258
8582               $579.00

xxxxxxxxxx2256

DEPOSIT TO CHECKING
000526899

125 JOE STREET
HEMM, IN
```

```
DATE ------

QUAN        DESC       AMOUNT
1           TOY         27.26

2356-85-1125-5698

KEVIN & SCOTT'S RAINY DAYS

Subtotal    27.26
Tax          1.23
TOTAL       28.49
```

RECORD ALL CHARGES OR CREDITS THAT AFFECT YOUR ACCOUNT

NUMBER	DATE	DESCRIPTION OF TRANSACTION	PAYMENT/DEBIT (−)	√ T	FEE (IF ANY)	DEPOSIT/CREDIT (+)	BALANCE $	

⌘ **Endorsing Checks**

Before you can cash or deposit a check written to you, it must be endorsed. To endorse a check means to sign your name on the back. The example shows a check written to Jim Burg. It also shows how he endorsed the check on the back. The check now can be cashed or deposited in Jim Burg's checking account.

Checks can be endorsed in different ways. If you have a check that you are going to deposit in your checking account, write "For Deposit Only," then your name. When you endorse it this way, it makes the check safe. If it were lost, no one could cash it. The check could only be put into your account. An example of this type of endorsement is shown below.

If you plan to cash the check, it is a good idea not to sign it at all until you get to the bank or ATM. That way, if you were to lose the check beforehand, it would be less likely that someone could pretend he or she was you and cash it. If you do lose a check, be sure to report that immediately to the person or business who gave it to you. Then the bank can stop payment on that check.

```
                                                      101
                                  Dec. 7    20 - -     71-587/749
PAY TO THE
ORDER OF    Jim Burg                          $  10.00
Ten and 00/100                                        DOLLARS

FIRST NATIONAL BANK

MEMO                             Jane Doe

⑆074905872⑆   251⑆372⑆8⑈   0101
```

| Jim Burg | For Deposit Only
Jim Burg |
| --- | --- |

⌘ Imagine you are Laura Nicole. Pictured below is a paycheck you received for some work you did. Show how you would endorse it to receive cash.

	124

Dec. 11 20 —   71-587/749

PAY TO THE ORDER OF   *Laura Nicole* $ *15.00*

Fifteen and 00/100 ———————— DOLLARS

FIRST NATIONAL BANK

MEMO ———————   *Jane Doe*

⑈074905872⑈   251⑈372⑈8‖⁣• 0124

⌘ Imagine you are Suneel Ratan. The following is a check received from a friend. You decided to put the full amount in your checking account. Endorse the check so no one else can cash it.

	301

Feb. 8 20 —   71-587/749

PAY TO THE ORDER OF   *Suneel Ratan* $ *25.00*

Twenty-five and 00/100 ———————— DOLLARS

FIRST NATIONAL BANK

MEMO ———————   *Quynh Thai*

⑈074905872⑈   251⑈372⑈8‖⁣• 0301

⌘ Bank Costs

Different banks have different charges. It is a good idea to shop around before you choose a bank. Some charges a bank might require are listed below.

Service charge—This is a payment that the bank deducts from your account for taking care of your money and paying the checks that you write. You will be charged this amount on the form the bank sends you at the end of each month. This form is called your statement. You need to subtract this amount from your check records.

HARRISON BANKING	
	For Better Banking Service
Service Charge	
$300.00 or less	$2.00 per month
$500.00 or less	$1.00 per month
$750.00 or less	$ .50 per month
Over $750.00	no charge

Minimum balance—Some banks charge you according to how much money you keep in an account. For instance, the minimum balance for no service charge might be $300.00. That means at least $300.00 must be in your account at all times to keep from paying an extra fee. Different amounts might cause you to be charged larger or smaller fees. Study the sample bank advertisement above.

Charge per check—Sometimes this type of account charges no service charge. You pay according to the number of checks that are written. For example, you could pay $.08 on each check written. If you write 15 checks in one month, the charge will be $1.20 ($.08 × 15 = $1.20). At other banks, you might pay a regular monthly service charge in addition to a charge per check.

Interest—Some banks pay interest, which is a fee paid for the use of your money. Usually you have to keep a certain minimum amount of money in your checking account in order to earn interest.

New checks—Every time you order new checks, there is a charge for them. The charge is usually taken from your checking account by the bank and is shown on your monthly statement. You then need to subtract this amount from your checkbook register.

Overdraft fee—This is a fee charged by the bank if you overdraw a bank account, called an overdraft. This amount might be $20.00 to $25.00 depending on the bank. If you write checks for a larger amount than you have in your account, you will be charged an overdraft fee. This amount will be subtracted from your account by the bank. Overdrafts are against the law, so the bank charges you this penalty. Call the bank if you find out that you made a mistake and overdrew your account. If you do not have enough money in your account to cover the check, the bank will return the check unpaid. This is bad for your credit rating. If you write a bad check to a store, the store itself may charge a returned-check fee that you must pay in addition to the bank's overdraft charge. The store may also decide not to accept checks from you in the future. If you bounce a check for a loan payment, credit card payment, or other important payments, your credit rating will suffer. This means that it will be difficult to obtain credit in the future.

Overdraft protection—Some banks offer overdraft protection. Money from a savings account can be moved to your checking account to cover the overdrawn amount. You must sign an overdraft card for this to take place. Ask your bank if they offer this service.

Debit and ATM Charges—Many banks charge you for using these two cards. A small fee, such as $.50 to $2.00, may be charged every time you use one of these cards. Remember to subtract this charge from your check record.

⌘ Finding the Best Bank

It is best to shop around when choosing a bank. The services banks offer can vary a great deal, as can the fees they charge. Most banks have pamphlets that explain all their services, fees, and policies. You can also get information on-line from banks' web sites. Compare information from different banks carefully. Then you can decide which would be the best bank for your needs. Study the two ads below. Choose the bank at which you would like to start your account.

Ad 1

Bank of Genessee

SERVICE CHARGE

$250 or less ....$4.00/mo.

$251-$500..$2.00/mo.

Over $500 ....none

Per-check charge: $.08.

$.50 charge per ATM use.

Ad 2

BANK OF BRYANT

SERVICE CHARGE

$200 or less ....$2.00/mo.

$201-$400..$1.00/mo.

Over $400 ....none

Per-check charge: first ten checks per month free; $.09 per check over ten.

$1.50 charge per ATM use.

Find the service charge and the cost of the new checks you ordered below. The top portion of a bank statement should tell you the total of the service charge. The example below is only the top portion of a bank statement. The bank statement will be studied later on in this book.

First National Bank

PREVIOUS STATEMENT 9/2/__, BALANCE OF 1097.43

6 DEPOSITS AND OTHER CREDITS TOTALING.....................4571.71+

45 CHECKS AND OTHER DEBITS TOTALING 3477.76–

SERVICE CHARGE...........................3.60–

NEW CHECKS ORDERED........................20.00–

BALANCE AS OF 9/30/__.....................2167.78

⌘ Figure the service charge you would pay if your bank charges you for each check:

May—21 checks at $.10 for each check.   _____

June—29 checks at $.09 for each check.   _____

July—12 checks at $.08 for each check.   _____

In July you wrote a check for $261.00. Your checking account only had $259.00 in it. The bank charged you for an overdraft (OD). How much did they charge? Look at the statement below. This is only a part of the bank statement. The overdraft will appear as an OD. The bank also charged an ATM charge. It is listed below the OD charge.

DATE	CK. NO	AMOUNT	DATE	CK. NO	AMOUNT
07/03	4560	5.30	07/16	4563	62.87
07/03	4520	16.32	07/18	4528	84.23
07/09	4523	152.00	07/20	4530	261.00
07/15	4562	68.89	07/20		20.00 OD
			07/20	ATM CHARGE	1.50

⌘ Lost Checks or ATM/Debit Cards

If you happen to lose some blank checks or your ATM or debit card, you should do the following:

❐ Call the bank immediately. Someone might try to use the checks or card.

❐ Give the bank the numbers of the lost checks or the ATM/debit card.

❐ If you find the checks or the card, notify the bank immediately.

The bank will watch for these checks and not pay them. Without your PIN and proper identification, it will be difficult for anyone to steal from your account. The bank will discontinue this card and issue a new one.

⌘ Reconciling Your Checking Account

At the end of each month, the bank will send you a statement. An activity statement, or bank statement, is the bank's record of your checks, deposits, ATM and debit card transactions, and any fees you might owe. You will use this information to balance your checkbook. On the following page is an example of a bank statement.

⌘ **Activity Statement**

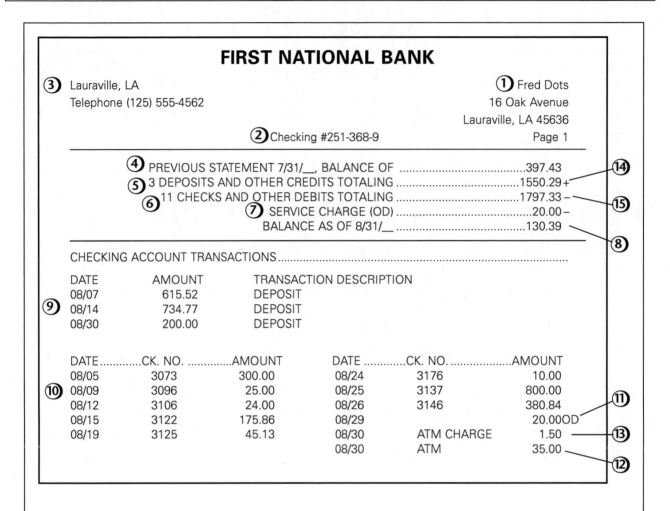

FIRST NATIONAL BANK

③ Lauraville, LA
Telephone (125) 555-4562

① Fred Dots
16 Oak Avenue
Lauraville, LA 45636

② Checking #251-368-9   Page 1

④ PREVIOUS STATEMENT 7/31/__, BALANCE OF ....397.43 ⑭
⑤ 3 DEPOSITS AND OTHER CREDITS TOTALING ....1550.29+
⑥ 11 CHECKS AND OTHER DEBITS TOTALING ....1797.33 – ⑮
⑦ SERVICE CHARGE (OD) ....20.00 –
BALANCE AS OF 8/31/__ ....130.39 ⑧

CHECKING ACCOUNT TRANSACTIONS...

DATE	AMOUNT	TRANSACTION DESCRIPTION
08/07	615.52	DEPOSIT
08/14	734.77	DEPOSIT
08/30	200.00	DEPOSIT

⑨

DATE	CK. NO.	AMOUNT	DATE	CK. NO.	AMOUNT
08/05	3073	300.00	08/24	3176	10.00
08/09	3096	25.00	08/25	3137	800.00
08/12	3106	24.00	08/26	3146	380.84
08/15	3122	175.86	08/29		20.00OD
08/19	3125	45.13	08/30	ATM CHARGE	1.50
			08/30	ATM	35.00

⑩   ⑪ ⑬ ⑫

Key

① Name and address of person(s) holding account

② Number of person's checking account

③ The bank's address and phone number

④ The amount left over from the month before

⑤ The number of deposits made this month

⑥ The number of checks written and other debits made this month

⑦ The amount of the service charge

⑧ The amount left over at the end of this month

⑨ The date and amount of each deposit made this month

⑩ The date, check number, and amount of each check written or ATM withdrawal made this month

⑪ The amount of the overdraft person had to pay

⑫ The amount of cash withdrawn from checking account at the ATM

⑬ Fee charged for using the ATM

⑭ The total of deposits made in this month

⑮ The total amount of checks written and other debits made in this month

⌘ Look at the bank statement below and answer the questions listed.

⌘ Activity Statement

FIRST NATIONAL BANK

Lauraville, LA   Your Name
Telephone (125) 555-4562   40 Park Street
                                                     Lauraville, LA 45637
                    Checking #251-382-9   Page 1

PREVIOUS STATEMENT 9/30/__, BALANCE OF 986.23
4 DEPOSITS AND OTHER CREDITS TOTALING ....1123.76+
12 CHECKS AND OTHER DEBITS TOTALING 1075.99–
SERVICE CHARGE (.08 PER CHECK) 80–
BALANCE AS OF 10/31/__ 1033.20

CHECKING ACCOUNT TRANSACTIONS...

DATE	AMOUNT	TRANSACTION DESCRIPTION
08/02	236.98	DEPOSIT
08/15	638.23	DEPOSIT
08/23	148.55	DEPOSIT
08/24	100.00	ATM DEPOSIT

DATE	CK. NO.	AMOUNT	DATE	CK. NO.	AMOUNT
10/05	3066	21.98	10/17	3071	19.76
10/09	3067	122.88	10/19	3072	5.00
10/09	3068	462.92	10/27	3073	160.92
10/10	3069	10.22	10/29	3074	155.00
10/13	3070	9.65	10/29	3075	32.56
			10/29	DEBIT	74.60
			10/31	ATM	.50

1. What was the ending balance for the last month? _____

2. On what day was check number 3066 cleared by the bank? _____

3. How many deposits did you make this month? _____

4. How many checks did you write? _____

5. What is the balance at the end of this month? _____

6. Is there a service charge this month? _____

7. Did you have an overdraft? _____

8. Was the amount $462.92 added or subtracted? _____

9. Was the service charge subtracted or added? _____

10. How much did you pay for writing a check? _____

11. Did you use your ATM card? _____

12. How much did you pay out on your debit card? _____

The back of the bank statement will look something like the example below. It will help you balance your checkbook.

⌘ **Balance Sheet**

This form will help you balance your bank statement.

The activity statement lists magnetically prenumbered checks in the order that you write them, not in the order the bank pays them. This saves you time as you do not need to sort checks. Simply refer to the check number column of the statement and mark off those checks paid on your check register. Checks that are not magnetically prenumbered are listed in the order the bank pays them and will need to be checked off your register also.

Any charges appearing on this statement but not appearing in your register should be deducted from your register balance before attempting to balance your register to this statement. Likewise, any credits appearing on this statement but not appearing in your register should be added to your register balance.

BANK BALANCE ②
shown on this statement $ _____

ADD + DEPOSITS ③ $ _____
made but not shown on
statement because made $ _____
or received after date of
this statement. $ _____

④ TOTAL $ _____

SUBTRACT –
CHECKS OUTSTANDING ⑤ $ _____

BALANCE ⑥
(Should agree with your
adjusted Register Balance) $ _____

① **CHECKS OUTSTANDING**
(Written but not shown on statement because not yet received by bank)

CHECK NUMBER	AMOUNT
TOTAL	

IN CASE OF ERROR OR QUESTION ABOUT YOUR ELECTRONIC TRANSACTION, CALL US AT 555-8965 OR WRITE TO US AT P.O. BOX 23, LAURAVILLE, LA.

Here is an explanation of the back of the activity statement. You will need to know these terms to help balance your checkbook.

① Checks Outstanding—This is the area where any checks you have written but the bank has not paid are listed. Put the numbers of the checks and the amounts here. Make sure you put in any debit card or ATM transaction that the bank does not show on the activity statement. These transactions should only be ones that have taken cash from your checking, transferred money out of your checking, or represent a debit payment to someone. All these items are then totaled and the amount put at the bottom.

② Bank Balance—This is the amount the bank says that you have in your account. You will find this number on the front of the bank statement under "Balance as of."

③ Deposits—Look at your deposit record. This may be in a separate book or written in the front of the checkbook. You may also have receipts given to you at the bank or ATM each time you make a deposit. It is a good idea to always record the ATM and debit deposits into the deposit record in the front of your check register. Compare the bank statement deposits shown on the front of the statement with the ones in your own records.

④ Total—Add the bank balance and any deposits not shown on the activity statement and place the amount on this line.

⑤ Subtract Checks Outstanding—The total of outstanding checks in the box on the right will be placed on this line. This amount will be subtracted from the "Total."

⑥ Balance—This is the amount you have in your checking account. This number should match the final number in your checkbook records.

NOTE: Be sure to subtract any service charge or ATM charges the bank requires you to pay from your checkbook records.

To begin reconciling, do the following steps:

1. Using your record book and the activity statement, make a check mark in the appropriate box headed √ T for each check shown as paid on your statement. Also checkmark the ATM and debit card transactions that are shown on the statement.

2. Look through your record book for any ATM or debit card transactions that are not shown on your statement or checks that were not paid by the bank. These will be easy to find, since you will have no check marks by these.

3. On the back of the bank statement is a place to help reconcile your checkbook. Begin by listing any outstanding checks or ATM and debit card transactions.

4. List the balance shown on the statement.

5. List any deposits made since then, and add this to the balance.

6. Subtract outstanding checks, ATM transactions, and debit card transactions.

7. Make sure a check record is not missing from your records. You might have written a check and not recorded it. Check all ATM and debit card transactions. Make sure they have all been recorded in your check register.

8. Subtract any service charge(s) from your checkbook.

9. The final amount should match the balance in your checkbook.

Following are examples of a bank statement and check register. Use the information given and reconcile the checking account using the balance sheet on page 30. Follow steps 1–9 to help you. The following are the deposits listed on the deposit record page. Be sure to compare them to the activity statement.

DEPOSIT RECORD				
6/1	85	L.R.	1184	00
6/10	85	J.R.	198	00
6/15	85	L.R.	236	00
6/25	85	L.R.	951	20
7/1	85	J.R.	754	12

⌘ Activity Statement

FIRST NATIONAL BANK

Lauraville, LA

Telephone (125) 555-4562

Fred Dots
16 Oak Avenue
Lauraville, LA 45636

Checking #251-382-9   Page 1

PREVIOUS STATEMENT 5/31/__, BALANCE OF 855.23
4 DEPOSITS AND OTHER CREDITS TOTALING 2569.20
10 CHECKS AND OTHER DEBITS TOTALING 2047.07
BALANCE AS OF 6/30/__ 1377.36

CHECKING ACCOUNT TRANSACTIONS..

DATE	AMOUNT	TRANSACTION DESCRIPTION
06/01	1184.00	DEPOSIT
06/10	198.00	DEPOSIT
06/15	236.00	DEPOSIT
06/25	951.20	DEPOSIT

DATE	CK. NO.	AMOUNT	DATE	CK. NO.	AMOUNT
06/02	1221	48.99	06/20	1228	11.82
06/04	1222	900.00	06/28	1229	5.43
06/10	1223	10.89	06/29	1230	316.55
06/11	1225	47.89	06/30	1231	606.44
06/15	1227	51.22	06/30	DEBIT	47.84

⌘ **Check Register Page**

RECORD ALL CHARGES OR CREDITS THAT AFFECT YOUR ACCOUNT

NUMBER	DATE	DESCRIPTION OF TRANSACTION	PAYMENT/DEBIT (–)		√ T	FEE (IF ANY)	DEPOSIT/CREDIT (+)		BALANCE $ 855	23
---	6/1	Deposit					1,184	00	1,184	--
									2,039	23
1221	6/2	John Smith	48	99					48	99
		car parts							1,990	24
1222	6/4	Davis T.V. Repair	900	00					900	00
		T.V. Fixed							1,090	24
1223	6/10	Alice's Sport Shop	10	89					10	89
		sweatbands							1,079	35
---	6/10	Deposit					198	00	198	00
									1,277	35
1224	6/11	Theresa's Grocery	9	82					9	82
		food							1,267	53
1225	6/11	Judy's Chops	47	89					47	89
		meat							1,219	64
1226	6/13	Loretta's Gift Shop	49	86					49	86
									1,169	78
---	6/15	Deposit					236	00	236	00
									1,405	78
1227	6/15	Remaklus Clothing	51	22					51	22
		slacks							1,354	56
1228	6/20	Laux Grocery	11	82					11	82
		food							1,342	74
---	6/25	Deposit					951	20	951	20
									2,293	94
1229	6/28	Renee's Dolls	5	43					5	43
		doll							2,288	51
1230	6/29	Bryant Mill	316	55					316	55
		animal feed							1,971	96
1231	6/30	Dexter and Mary's Supplies	606	44					606	44
		lumber							1,365	52
Debit	6/30	Julie's Flowers	47	84					47	84
									1,317	68
---	7/1	Deposit					754	12	754	12
									2,071	80
ATM	7/1	Cash	45	00					45	00
									2,026	80
		ATM Charge				.85				85
									2,025	95

⌘ **Balance Sheet**

This form will help you balance your bank statement.

The activity statement lists magnetically prenumbered checks in the order that you write them, not in the order the bank pays them. This saves you time as you do not need to sort checks. Simply refer to the check number column of the statement and mark off those checks paid on your check register. Checks that are not magnetically prenumbered are listed in the order the bank pays them and will need to be checked off your register also.

Any charges appearing on this statement but not appearing in your register should be deducted from your register balance before attempting to balance your register to this statement. Likewise, any credits appearing on this statement but not appearing in your register should be added to your register balance.

BANK BALANCE
shown on this statement $ _____

ADD + DEPOSITS
made but not shown on $ _____
statement because made
or received after date of $ _____
this statement. $ _____

                              TOTAL $ _____

SUBTRACT –
CHECKS OUTSTANDING $ _____

BALANCE
(Should agree with your
adjusted Register Balance) $ _____

CHECKS OUTSTANDING
(Written but not shown on statement
because not yet received by bank)

CHECK NUMBER	AMOUNT
TOTAL	

IN CASE OF ERROR OR QUESTION ABOUT YOUR ELECTRONIC TRANSACTION, CALL US AT 555-8965 OR WRITE TO US AT P.O. BOX 23, LAURAVILLE, LA.

⌘ Making Your Records Agree

Sometimes you might have problems getting your records to agree. Here are a few things to look for if you have problems.

- ❏ Make sure you subtracted from your check records any service charge, check fee, or ATM/debit card fee the bank might have charged.

- ❏ Check all deposits. Make sure you added all deposits to your records. Also check to see if any deposits were made after the statement came. You would have to add these on the back of the activity statement. Don't forget to check any deposits that you made at the automated teller machine.

- ❏ Look again for any outstanding checks. Make sure they are all listed and subtracted from the activity statement. Don't forget about your debit card. All activity should have been written in your check register.

- ❏ Make sure a check record is not missing from your register. You might have written a check and not recorded it.

- ❏ If none of the above seem to be the problem, you need to go over your addition and subtraction in the record book and on the back of the activity statement. Small errors can happen.

⌘ Keeping Track of Expenses

A budget is an organized plan for spending money. This plan will help you set aside money for mortgage, rent payments, or any bill that you pay regularly. It will also be a plan for expenses that you do not pay regularly, such as money for trips or a new outfit to wear. These expenses are known as expenditures. By keeping track of what you spend, you can see if your take-home pay will cover all expenditures. It will help you prepare a budget for needed items as well as luxuries.

Your check register is a real help in tracking expenses. If you pay your bills by check, your check register will show you how much you spend. You should also try to keep track of any cash you take out when you deposit your paycheck.

There are many forms, books, and on-line resources that can help you plan your money needs. You can easily make a monthly expense form of your own. On the next page is an example of a monthly expense form. On the page following that is a list of expenses and other items you can enter on this form for practice.

⌘ Monthly Expenses—January

FOOD.. $ _____

HOUSING

Rent (House Payment) .... $ _____

Insurance .... $ _____

Home Repairs .... $ _____

Furniture Payments .... $ _____

Phone..................................... $ _____

Water .... $ _____

Gas/Oil .... $ _____

Electricity .... $ _____

Appliances .... $ _____

Other...................................... $ _____

TOTAL $ _____

HEALTH CARE

Doctor .... $ _____

Hospital.................................. $ _____

X rays, Glasses .... $ _____

Medicine................................ $ _____

Insurance .... $ _____

Dentist .... $ _____

TOTAL $ _____

CLOTHING

New .... $ _____

Cleaning/Repair..................... $ _____

TOTAL $ _____

TRANSPORTATION

Car Payment.......................... $ _____

Car Repair .... $ _____

Gas/Oil .... $ _____

License .... $ _____

Insurance .... $ _____

Bus/Cab .... $ _____

TOTAL $ _____

LIFE INSURANCE .... $ _____

MISCELLANEOUS

Haircut .... $ _____

Baby-sitter............................. $ _____

Hobbies.................................. $ _____

Trips .... $ _____

Gifts .... $ _____

Personal Needs .... $ _____

Recreation.............................. $ _____

Bank/ATM Service Charges .... $ _____

Petty Cash .... $ _____

Other...................................... $ _____

TOTAL $ _____

SAVINGS .... $ _____

HOLIDAY CLUB .... $ _____

VACATION CLUB .... $ _____

TOTAL EXPENDITURES .... $ _____

MONTHLY TAKE-HOME PAY

Paycheck................................ $ _____

Spouse................................... $ _____

Other Income .... $ _____

TOTAL $ _____

Watch to see if your income is less than your expenditures. If this happens, you must make cuts somewhere. If your income is more than your expenditures, you've done a great job!

Note: You need to add some weekly amounts to get the total for the month of some items. Example: Food—1st week, $43.50; 2nd week, $51.88; 3rd week, $43.62; and 4th week, $31.22. The total for the month is $170.22.

⌘ Fill in the Monthly Expenses form on page 32 with the following information:

Your salary each week is $325.00. You will have four paydays in the month. A birthday gift of $25.00 was also given to you.

Here are your expenses for the month of January:

Rent	$534.00	for the month
Phone	$ 43.22	for the month
Electricity	$ 99.82	for the month
Glasses	$ 42.00	for the month
Clothing	$ 24.99	for the month
Food	$ 43.50	1st week
	$ 51.88	2nd week
	$ 43.62	3rd week
	$ 31.22	4th week
Car Payment	$242.00	for the month
Gas	$ 14.00	1st week
	$ 20.00	2nd week
	$ 15.00	3rd week
	$ 17.00	4th week
Movie	$ 4.00	1st week
	$ 8.00	2nd week
	$ 8.00	3rd week
Savings	$ 35.00	1st week
	$ 35.00	2nd week

Remember to total the weeks' amounts and put the total for the month in the proper place.

Part 2:
Six-Month
Banking Simulation

⌘ Introduction

Now that you know how a checking account works, you're going to practice handling one. On the following pages you will be writing checks, filling out deposit slips, maintaining a checkbook register, recording ATM and debit slips, balancing a checkbook, and keeping track of expenses. If you have any questions, refer to the work you did in Part 1: Understanding Your Checking Account.

Each week of the simulation, you will "receive" a paycheck to deposit. You may also "receive" other miscellaneous checks. Record your deposits on your deposit record sheet, and add them to the balance on your check register.

You will also have weekly and monthly bills, such as electricity, telephone, and rent. Write checks to pay your bills. Then subtract the checks from the balance on your check register. Don't forget to record the ATM or debit card transactions. At the end of the month, make sure that your records agree with the bank's records. Compare your check register to the activity statement for that month. Use the form provided to reconcile your account.

Finally, record all expenses and income on the monthly expenses sheet.

For the first month of the simulation, the checks are printed underneath the bills you need to pay. For the other months, use the blank checks printed at the back of the book. The other forms you will need—deposit slips, deposit records, and check register pages—are also printed at the back of the book. If you need more of any of these forms, your teacher will give them to you. As you work through the simulation, remember to add deposits on your register sheet, and to subtract checks.

To start working on this banking exercise, make the following deposit:

Month of January ———————————————————

Week No. 1
Deposit—January 7, 20 ___

❏ one payroll check, $465.00

❏ one check for $130.00 for some used furniture you sold

❏ one check for $5.00 you won in a contest

Request $50.00 back in cash. Use $35.00 of this cash for car gasoline. The remaining $15 you can keep track of under "Petty Cash" on your monthly expense sheet. (Petty cash is the cash you get back when you deposit your check. You may use petty cash for various small expenses. In this simulation, the cash is not accounted for in any other way. If the simulation requests that you make an ATM cash withdrawal for a specific purpose, record the expenditure in an appropriate space on the expense sheet. If no specific purpose is given, then list it under "Petty cash.")

Use the given dates on all deposit slips and checks. Always check the bills to see if they have been added correctly.

⌘ **CHECK NO. 101** | January 7, 20__

MWP MIDWESTERN PHONE

P.O. BOX 1980, JULIES, LA • BUSINESS OFFICE: 555-9873

PAGE 1
DATE OF BILL
12/01/—
12/31/—

Exchange: LAURAVILLE		REF.	DATE	TIME	TOLLS	AMOUNT
TEL. NO. 555-9876		01	12/02	0453	Celina	.62
		02	12/04	0429	Green	.48
		03	12/05	0637	Wabach	1.16
Your Name		04	12/06	0717	Bryant	5.99
40 Park Street		05	12/08	0802	Honolulu	5.37
Lauraville, LA 45637						

LOCAL SERVICE	OTHER CHARGES	TOLLS	STATE TAX	FEDERAL TAX	PREVIOUS BAL. DUE	TOTAL BILL DUE
10.26	0.00	13.62	.98	.96	0.00	25.82

101

_____ 20 _____ 71-587/749

PAY TO THE
ORDER OF _____ $ _____

_____ DOLLARS

FIRST NATIONAL BANK

MEMO _____ _____

⑈074905872⑈   251⑈372⑈8⑈   0101

⌘ **CHECK NO. 102** | January 7, 20__
You go grocery shopping and write a check for $60.82 to Laux Grocery for food.

102

_____ 20 _____ 71-587/749

PAY TO THE
ORDER OF _____ $ _____

_____ DOLLARS

FIRST NATIONAL BANK

MEMO _____ _____

⑈074905872⑈   251⑈372⑈8⑈   0102

⌘ **CHECK NO. 103** | January 8, 20__

PENNVILLEE, LA.

LAURA'S CLOTHING STORE

INVOICE					
SOLD BY:		CASH	CHARGE	ON ACCOUNT	
Quantity	Description			Price	Amount
1	Jeans				$21.21

Keep this slip for REFERENCE.

103

_____ 20 _____   71-587/749

PAY TO THE
ORDER OF _____ $ _____

_____ DOLLARS

FIRST NATIONAL BANK

MEMO _____   _____

⑆074905872⑆   251⑆372⑆8⑆ 0103

⌘ **DEBIT CARD TRANSACTION** | January 9, 20__
See debit receipt below.

```
MUHLENKAMP'S BOAT MARINA

DATE 01/09/-
2518-95-1125-5896

QUAN    DESC      AMOUNT
   1    Boat Rental  40.23

        Subtotal    40.23
        Tax          2.57
        TOTAL       42.80
```

⌘ **CHECK NO. 104** | January 10, 20___
The stone quarry delivered a small load of gravel for the walkway.

Regent Bros. Stone Quarry
BRYANT, LA 45983 · PHONE 555-6525

DESCRIPTION OF ITEM	PRICE	AMOUNT	
#10		$75	75
	TAX	4.25	
	TOTAL	$80.00	

104

_____ 20 ____   71-587/749

PAY TO THE
ORDER OF _____ $ _____

_____ DOLLARS

FIRST NATIONAL BANK

MEMO _____

⑆074905872⑆   251⑈372⑈8⑆   0104

⌘ **CHECK NO. 105** | January 10, 20___
You run out of milk. Write a check for $5.42 to Laux Grocery for the items you buy.

105

_____ 20 ____   71-587/749

PAY TO THE
ORDER OF _____ $ _____

_____ DOLLARS

FIRST NATIONAL BANK

MEMO _____

⑆074905872⑆   251⑈372⑈8⑆   0105

Week No. 2
Deposit—January 14, 20___

❐ one payroll check, $465.00

❐ one check for $25.00 (This was a gift from your aunt.)

Request $50.00 back in cash. Use $30.00 of this cash for car gasoline.

⌘ **CHECK NO. 106** | January 15, 20__

Payment No. 1		Payment No.	Account No.	Due	Amount Due
		1	251-368-9	1/15	$572.95
Date _____					
Ck. No. _____		**FIRST NATIONAL BANK**			
Amount _____		LAURAVILLE, LA			
		Real Estate			
KEEP THIS PART FOR YOUR RECORDS.		IMPORTANT: THIS COUPON SHOULD ACCOMPANY PAYMENT.			

106

_____ 20 _____ 71-587/749

PAY TO THE
ORDER OF _____ $ _____

_____ DOLLARS

FIRST NATIONAL BANK

MEMO _____ _____

⑈074905872⑈ 251⑈372⑈8⑈ ⑈0106

⌘ **CHECK NO. 107** | January 16, 20__

READ METER NOW			KEEP FOR YOUR RECORDS	Your Name
JAY COUNTY RURAL ELECTRIC			Meter No. 1452 WE	40 Park Street Lauraville, LA 45637
			Acct. No. 00-003-085	RETURN THIS COPY WITH PAYMENT

From Reading	To Reading	KWH Used	Amount Due		KWH USED	METER RD.
13480	15300	1820	$ 98.11		1820	----------------
Mo.	**Day**	**Yr.**	**Net Bill**			
12	01	__	$ 98.11			
Mo.	**Day**	**Yr.**	**Bill w/Penalty**		TOTAL AMOUNT DUE	
12	31	__	$101.98		$98.11	

107

_____ 20 _____   71-587/749

PAY TO THE
ORDER OF _____ $ _____

_____ D O L L A R S

FIRST NATIONAL BANK

MEMO _____   _____

⑆074905872⑆   251⑈372⑉8⑈   0107

⌘ **CHECK NO. 108** | January 17, 20__
You need some medicine for your cold. Write a check for $7.86 to Wingate's Pharmacy for medicine.

108

_____ 20 _____   71-587/749

PAY TO THE
ORDER OF _____ $ _____

_____ D O L L A R S

FIRST NATIONAL BANK

MEMO _____   _____

⑆074905872⑆   251⑈372⑉8⑈   0108

✣ **CHECK NO. 109** | January 17, 20__

TOM'S BOOT REPAIR
COLDWATER, LA

DESCRIPTION	PRICE	AMOUNT
Heel Replaced	*$2.25*	*$2.25*

	109
	_____ 20 _____ 71-587/749
PAY TO THE ORDER OF _____	$ _____
_____ DOLLARS
FIRST NATIONAL BANK	
MEMO _____	
⑆074905872⑆ 251⑈372⑈8⑈ 0109	

✣ **CHECK NO. 110** | January 18, 20__
Julie Nicole babysat your dog. Write a check to her for $6.00.

	110
	_____ 20 _____ 71-587/749
PAY TO THE ORDER OF _____	$ _____
_____ DOLLARS
FIRST NATIONAL BANK	
MEMO _____	
⑆074905872⑆ 251⑈372⑈8⑈ 0110	

Week No. 3
Deposit—January 21, 20 ___

❑ one payroll check, $465.00

❑ three $20 bills

❑ two $10 bills

❑ eighteen quarters

⌘ **CHECK NO. 111** | January 21, 20__

KEEP THIS STUB	**SRLC**	**S.R. Loan Co.** AUTO LOAN	**Payment No.** 1 DUE DATE 1/22
PAYMENT NO: 1		❖ *S.R. Loan Company*	
		MAKE CHECKS PAYABLE TO: SRLC	
AMOUNT DUE: $245.00		Return this stub with payment.	**TOTAL DUE** $245.00

111

_____ 20 _____   71-587/749

PAY TO THE
ORDER OF _____ $ _____

_____ DOLLARS

FIRST NATIONAL BANK

MEMO _____   _____

⑈074905872⑈   251⑈372⑈8⑈' 0111

✤ **CHECK NO. 112** | January 22, 20__
The water bill is due. Write the check to County Water Works for $21.67.

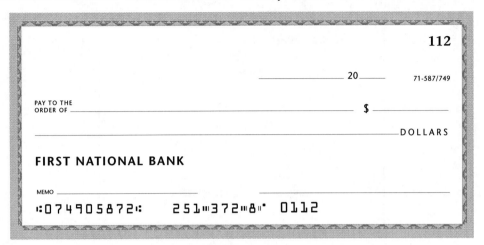

✤ **CHECK NO. 113** | January 23, 20__
You had your hair cut. Write a check for $12.50 to Julie's Chop Shop.

✤ **CHECK NO. 114** | January 23, 20__
You need groceries. Write a check to Laux Grocery for $29.61.

⌘ **DEBIT CARD TRANSACTION** | January 23, 20__
See debit receipt below.

```
DATE 01/23/-

2518-95-1125-5896

                DESC    AMOUNT
                GROCERIES 5.62
        TOTAL             5.62



            DEAN'S GROCERY
```

⌘ **CHECK NO. 115** | January 23, 20__
Your car needed work. The following bill needs to be paid.

Linda, LA

Zehringer Body Shop

DESCRIPTION OF REPAIR	COST		TOTAL AMOUNT	
Filter Replaced (labor)	$ 25	00	$ 25	00
Parts	$ 32	18	32	18
Total			$ 57	18

	115

_____ 20 _____   71-587/749

PAY TO THE
ORDER OF _____ $ _____

_____ DOLLARS

FIRST NATIONAL BANK

MEMO _____   _____

⑆074905872⑆   251⑈372⑈8⑈   0115

⌘ **CHECK NO. 116** | January 25, 20__
You decide to fertilize your lawn. Pay $25.85 to Windy's Lawn Supplies.

```
                                                              116

                                      _____ 20 _____    71-587/749

PAY TO THE
ORDER OF _____    $ _____

_____ DOLLARS

FIRST NATIONAL BANK

MEMO _____    _____
  ⑈074905872⑈    251⑈372⑈8⑈  0116
```

⌘ **ATM TRANSACTION** | January 25, 20__
See ATM receipt. You won this amount in a radio contest.

```
   0125-         0544PM      BE1258
                            $75.00

   xxxxxxxxx5896

   DEPOSIT TO CHECKING
   000258699


   125 JOE STREET
   WAGNER, LA
```

⌘ CHECK NO. 117 | January 25, 20__

Return with payment

Your Name
40 Park St.
Lauraville, LA

Policy No. 8102382
Premium Due $52.82

DETACH AND KEEP FOR YOUR RECORDS.

INSURED
Your Name
Premium for 06 mos.

POLICY NO.
8102382

Make check payable to:
M.R. LIFE INSURANCE

117

______ 20____ 71-587/749

PAY TO THE ORDER OF ______________________ $ ________

______________________ DOLLARS

FIRST NATIONAL BANK

MEMO ____________ ____________

⑆074905872⑆ 251⑈372⑈8⑈ 0117

Week No. 4

Deposit—January 28, 20 ___

❒ one payroll check, $465.00

Request $25.00 back in cash. Use $10.00 of this for car gasoline.
Put $5.00 of this in savings.

CHECK NO. 118 | January 29, 20__

⌘ You are invited to a wedding. At Loretta's Gift Shoppe you bought a crystal bowl, wrapping paper, and a bow. The total cost was $53.64. Write a check to cover these expenses.

118

______ 20____ 71-587/749

PAY TO THE ORDER OF ______________________ $ ________

______________________ DOLLARS

FIRST NATIONAL BANK

MEMO ____________ ____________

⑆074905872⑆ 251⑈372⑈8⑈ 0118

⌘ **CHECK NO. 119** | January 30, 20___
Your suit needed to be dry-cleaned for the wedding. Write a check for $11.32 to
Ranly Dry-Cleaners.

	119
	_____ 20 _____ 71-587/749
PAY TO THE ORDER OF _____	$ _____
_____ DOLLARS	
FIRST NATIONAL BANK	
MEMO _____	_____

⑈074905872⑈   251ⅲ372ⅲ8ⅱ 0119

⌘ **CHECK NO. 120** | January 30, 20___
You need groceries. Pay $25.37 to Judy's Market.

	120
	_____ 20 _____ 71-587/749
PAY TO THE ORDER OF _____	$ _____
_____ DOLLARS	
FIRST NATIONAL BANK	
MEMO _____	_____

⑈074905872⑈   251ⅲ372ⅲ8ⅱ 0120

⌘ **CHECK NO. 121** | January 31, 20__

ITEM	AMOUNT
Linen Shirt w/ Tax	*$41.91*
Total	*$41.91*

```
                                                    121
                            _____ 20 _____    71-587/749

PAY TO THE
ORDER OF _____  $ _____

_____ D O L L A R S

FIRST NATIONAL BANK

MEMO _____        _____
⑆074905872⑆    251⑈372⑈8⑈ 0121
```

⌘ **DEBIT CARD TRANSACTION** | January 31, 20__

Use your debit card to pay the following bill:

—————— *JACK'S BEACH SHOP* ——————

Clearwater Shores

Boat rental
3 hours .... TOTAL DUE: $60.00

This is the end of the month. Reconcile your bank account. If you have any questions, refer to Part 1: Understanding Your Checking Account.

Use the January bank statement, the balance sheet, the check register, and the monthly expenses form. Use the glossary for any words that you do not understand. After you have your checkbook balanced, you are ready to begin working on the month of February.

On a separate sheet, list and subtotal individual January expenditures for gas, clothing, food, trips, and so forth, as well as service charges and petty cash (cash back from paychecks and other deposits). Also keep track of other income (prizes, gifts, payment for odd jobs, and so forth).

⌘ **Activity Statement—January**

FIRST NATIONAL BANK

Lauraville, LA

Telephone:

(125) 555-4562

Your Name

40 Park Street

Lauraville, LA 45637

January

Page 1

Checking #251-372-8

PREVIOUS STATEMENT, NEW BALANCE OF 0.00

5 DEPOSITS AND OTHER CREDITS TOTALING 2054.50

20 CHECKS AND OTHER DEBITS TOTALING 1143.95

SERVICE CHARGE 1.00

BALANCE AS OF 1/31/— 909.55

CHECKING ACCOUNT TRANSACTIONS...

DATE	AMOUNT	TRANSACTION DESCRIPTION
JAN. 7	550.00	DEPOSIT
JAN. 14	440.00	DEPOSIT
JAN. 21	549.50	DEPOSIT
JAN. 25	75.00	ATM DEPOSIT
JAN. 28	440.00	DEPOSIT

DATE	CK. NO.	AMOUNT	DATE	CK. NO.	AMOUNT
JAN. 7	101	25.82	JAN. 22	112	21.67
JAN. 7	102	60.82	JAN. 23	113	12.50
JAN. 8	103	21.21	JAN. 23	114	29.61
JAN. 9	DEBIT	42.80	JAN. 23	DEBIT	5.62
JAN. 10	104	80.00	JAN. 23	115	57.18
JAN. 10	105	5.42	JAN. 29	118	53.64
JAN. 15	106	572.95	JAN. 30	119	11.32
JAN. 17	108	7.86	JAN. 30	120	25.37
JAN. 17	109	2.25	JAN. 31	121	41.91
JAN. 18	110	6.00	JAN. 31	DEBIT	60.00

DAILY BALANCE

DATE	AMOUNT	DATE	AMOUNT
JAN. 7	463.36	JAN. 21	714.37
JAN. 8	442.15	JAN. 22	692.70
JAN. 9	399.35	JAN. 23	587.79
JAN. 10	313.93	JAN. 25	662.79
JAN. 14	753.93	JAN. 28	1102.79
JAN. 15	180.98	JAN. 29	1049.15
JAN. 17	170.87	JAN. 30	1012.46
JAN. 18	164.87	JAN. 31	909.55

⌘ **Balance Sheet—January**

This form will help you balance your checkbook.

The activity statement lists magnetically prenumbered checks in the order that you write them, not in the order the bank pays them. This saves you time as you do not need to sort checks. Simply refer to the check number column of the statement and mark off those checks paid on your check register. Checks that are not magnetically prenumbered are listed in the order the bank pays them and will need to be checked off your register also.

Any charges appearing on this statement but not appearing in your register should be deducted from your register balance before attempting to balance your register to this statement. Likewise, any credits appearing on this statement but not appearing in your register should be added to your register balance.

BANK BALANCE
shown on this statement $ _____

ADD + DEPOSITS $ _____
made but not shown on
statement because made $ _____
or received after date of
this statement. $ _____

                          TOTAL $ _____

**SUBTRACT –
CHECKS OUTSTANDING** $ _____

BALANCE
(Should agree with your
adjusted Register Balance) $ _____

CHECKS OUTSTANDING
(Written but not shown on statement
because not yet received by bank)

CHECK NUMBER	AMOUNT
TOTAL	

IN CASE OF ERROR OR QUESTION ABOUT YOUR ELECTRONIC TRANSACTION, CALL US AT 555-8965 OR WRITE TO US AT P.O. BOX 23, LAURAVILLE, LA.

⌘ **Monthly Expenses—January**

FOOD......................... $ _____

HOUSING

Rent (House Payment) .... $ _____

Insurance .... $ _____

Home Repairs .... $ _____

Furniture Payments .... $ _____

Phone.................................... $ _____

Water .... $ _____

Gas/Oil .... $ _____

Electricity .... $ _____

Appliances .... $ _____

Other..................................... $ _____

TOTAL $ _____

HEALTH CARE

Doctor .... $ _____

Hospital................................. $ _____

X rays, Glasses .... $ _____

Medicine................................ $ _____

Insurance .... $ _____

Dentist .... $ _____

TOTAL $ _____

CLOTHING

New .... $ _____

Cleaning/Repair..................... $ _____

TOTAL $ _____

TRANSPORTATION

Car Payment.......................... $ _____

Car Repair .... $ _____

Gas/Oil.................................. $ _____

License .... $ _____

Insurance .... $ _____

Bus/Cab .... $ _____

TOTAL $ _____

LIFE INSURANCE .... $ _____

MISCELLANEOUS

Haircut .... $ _____

Baby-sitter............................. $ _____

Hobbies................................. $ _____

Trips .... $ _____

Gifts .... $ _____

Personal Needs .... $ _____

Recreation............................. $ _____

Bank/ATM Service Charges .... $ _____

Petty Cash .... $ _____

Other..................................... $ _____

TOTAL $ _____

SAVINGS .... $ _____

HOLIDAY CLUB .... $ _____

VACATION CLUB .... $ _____

TOTAL EXPENDITURES .... $ _____

MONTHLY TAKE-HOME PAY

Paycheck................................ $ _____

Spouse................................... $ _____

Other Income .... $ _____

TOTAL $ _____

Watch to see if your income is less than your expenditures. If this happens, you must make cuts somewhere. If your income is more than your expenditures, you've done a great job!

Month of February

Week No. 1

Deposit—February 1, 20___

❏ one payroll check, $465.00

Request $100.00 back in cash. Put $50.00 in your savings account and $25.00 in your Holiday Club account.

⌘ **CHECK NO. 122** | February 6, 20__

MW MIDWESTERN PHONE

P.O. BOX 1980, JULIES, LA • BUSINESS OFFICE: 555-9873

PAGE 1
DATE OF BILL
01/01/—
01/31/—

Exchange: LAURAVILLE TEL. NO. 555-9876	REF.	DATE	TIME	TOLLS	AMOUNT
	01	1/01	0235	Genenen	1.11
	02	1/05	0539	Blooms	.51
Your Name	03	1/08	0825	Minton	1.31
40 Park Street	04	1/23	1225	Genenen	1.12
Lauraville, LA 45637					

LOCAL SERVICE	OTHER CHARGES	TOLLS	STATE TAX	FEDERAL TAX	PREVIOUS BAL. DUE	TOTAL BILL DUE
10.26	0.00	4.05	.60	.52	0.00	15.43

⌘ **CHECK NO. 123** | February 8, 20__
You buy an antique dish for your collection from a friend. Pay Joseph Curran $15.00.

⌘ **CHECK NO. 124** | February 8, 20__
The kitchen woodwook needs painting. Write a check to Kaye's Paint Supplies for $19.50.

⌘ **ATM TRANSACTION** | February 9, 20__
See ATM receipt. You loaned cash to Renee. She will pay you back later.

```
02/09/--      0925AM      BE1258
8582                      $30.00

xxxxxxxxx5896

CASH
0052899621

9895 JAY STREET
CHRISTMAS, LA
```

Week No. 2

Deposit—February 11, 20___

❑ one payroll check, $465.00

❑ one check for $145.00 for a used stereo system you sold

Request $10.00 back in cash.

⌘ **CHECK NO. 125** | February 12, 20__
You need food. Write a check for $39.96 to Karch Grocer.

⌘ **CHECK NO. 126** | February 14, 20__

REINHART CLINIC

BORDER TOWN, LA

DATE	AMOUNT
Feb. 14	$123.95
TOTAL DUE	$123.95

⌘ **DEBIT CARD TRANSACTION** | February 14, 20__
See debit receipt.

```
DATE 0214--

QUAN          DESC      AMOUNT
1         MOWER BLADES   28.63

2518-95-1125-5896

TOTAL      $28.63

HAROLD'S REPAIR SHOP
```

⌘ **CHECK NO. 127** | February 15, 20__

Payment No. 2		Payment No.	Account No.	Due	Amount Due
		2	251-368-9	2/15	$572.95
Date _____					
Ck. No. _____		**FIRST NATIONAL BANK**			
Amount _____		LAURAVILLE, LA			
		Real Estate			
KEEP THIS PART FOR YOUR RECORDS		IMPORTANT: THIS COUPON SHOULD ACCOMPANY PAYMENT.			

⌘ **CHECK NO. 128** | February 16, 20__

READ METER NOW   KEEP FOR YOUR RECORDS

JAY COUNTY RURAL ELECTRIC

Your Name
40 Park Street
Lauraville, LA 45637

Meter No. 1452 WE
Acct. No. 00-003-085

RETURN THIS COPY WITH PAYMENT

From Reading	To Reading	KWH Used	Amount Due
15300	17030	1730	$ 82.76
Mo.	**Day**	**Yr.**	**Net Bill**
1	01	—	$ 82.76
Mo.	**Day**	**Yr.**	**Bill w/Penalty**
1	31	—	$ 98.77

KWH USED 1730   METER RD. ----------------

TOTAL AMOUNT DUE
$ 82.76

Week No. 3

Deposit—February 18, 20____

☐ one payroll check, $465.00

Get $50 back in cash. Put $20 in your savings account and $10 in your Holiday Club account.

⌘ **CHECK NO. 129** | February 19, 20__
Write a check for $10.00 to the United Way.

⌘ **CHECK NO. 130** | February 21, 20__

KEEP THIS STUB	**SRLC**	**S.R. Loan Co.** AUTO LOAN	**Payment No.** 2 DUE DATE 2/22
PAYMENT NO: 2	❖ *S.R. Loan Company*		
	MAKE CHECKS PAYABLE TO: SRLC		
AMOUNT DUE: $245.00	Return this stub with payment.		**TOTAL DUE** $245.00

⌘ **CHECK NO. 131** | February 22, 20__
The water bill is due. Write the check to County Water Works for $17.42.

Week No. 4

Deposit—February 25, 20__

❒ one payroll check, $465.00

❒ one check for $35.00 for the aluminum you collected

Request $100.00 back in cash. Put $50.00 in your Vacation Club account and $25.00 in your savings account. Use $5.00 of this for gas.

⌘ **CHECK NO. 132** | February 26, 20__
Write a check to Karch Grocer for $10.98.

⌘ **DEBIT CARD TRANSACTION** | February 27, 20__
See debit receipt.

```
DATE 0227--

QUAN          DESC          AMOUNT


2518-95-1125-5896

TOTAL        $23.78

CATHY'S PHARMACY
```

⌘ **CHECK NO. 133** | February 28, 20__

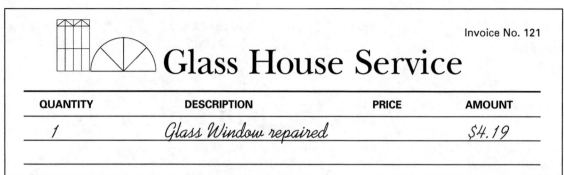

Invoice No. 121

Glass House Service

QUANTITY	DESCRIPTION	PRICE	AMOUNT
1	*Glass Window repaired*		*$4.19*

⌘ **CHECK NO. 134** | February 28, 20__
Write a check to Laux Grocery for $8.27.

⌘ **ATM TRANSACTION** | February 28, 20__
See ATM receipt. This was a rebate from the computer you bought a few months ago.

```
0228--        1010PM      BE1258
8582                      $45.00

xxxxxxxxxx5896

DEPOSIT TO CHECKING
0002568999

9856 ANDREW DR
DANNY, LA
```

⌘ **DEBIT CARD TRANSACTION** | February 28, 20__
Use your debit card to pay the following bill:

Lily's Record Store
Wilson Mall, West Lafayette

1 DVD	19.00
1 DVD	19.00
	38.00
tax	2.28
total	40.28

This is the end of the month. Follow the steps for reconciling your bank statement. Use the February bank statement, the balance sheet, the check register, and the monthly expenses form. Use the glossary for any words that you do not understand. After balancing your checkbook, continue with the next month of the simulation.

On a separate sheet list and subtotal individual February expenditures for gas, clothing, food, trips, and so forth, as well as service charges and petty cash (cash back from paychecks and other deposits). Also keep track of other income (prizes, gifts, payment for odd jobs, and so forth).

⌘ **Activity Statement—February**

FIRST NATIONAL BANK

Lauraville, LA
Telephone:
(125) 555-4562

Your Name
40 Park Street
Lauraville, LA 45637

February
Page 1

Checking #251-372-8

PREVIOUS STATEMENT , NEW BALANCE OF 909.55
4 DEPOSITS AND OTHER CREDITS TOTALING 1780.00
18 CHECKS AND OTHER DEBITS TOTALING 1509.33
SERVICE CHARGE .... .91
BALANCE AS OF 2/28/— 1179.31

CHECKING ACCOUNT TRANSACTIONS..

DATE	AMOUNT	TRANSACTION DESCRIPTION
FEB. 1	365.00	DEPOSIT
FEB. 11	600.00	DEPOSIT
FEB. 18	415.00	DEPOSIT
FEB. 25	400.00	DEPOSIT

DATE	CK. NO.	AMOUNT	DATE	CK. NO.	AMOUNT
JAN. 16	107	98.11	FEB. 15	127	572.95
JAN. 21	111	245.00	FEB. 16	128	82.76
JAN. 25	116	25.85	FEB. 19	129	10.00
FEB. 6	122	15.43	FEB. 21	130	245.00
FEB. 8	123	15.00	FEB. 22	131	17.42
FEB. 8	124	19.50	FEB. 26	132	10.98
FEB. 9	ATM	30.00	FEB. 28	133	4.19
FEB. 12	125	39.96	FEB. 28	134	8.27
FEB. 14	DEBIT	28.63	FEB. 28	DEBIT	40.28

DAILY BALANCE

DATE	AMOUNT	DATE	AMOUNT
BALANCE	909.55	FEB. 16	701.36
FEB. 1	905.59	FEB. 18	1116.36
FEB. 6	890.16	FEB. 19	1106.36
FEB. 8	855.66	FEB. 21	861.36
FEB. 9	825.66	FEB. 22	843.94
FEB. 11	1425.66	FEB. 25	1243.94
FEB. 12	1385.70	FEB. 26	1232.96
FEB. 14	1357.07	FEB. 28	1179.31
FEB. 15	784.12		

⌘ **Balance Sheet—February**

This form will help you balance your bank statement.

The activity statement lists magnetically prenumbered checks in the order that you write them, not in the order the bank pays them. This saves you time as you do not need to sort checks. Simply refer to the check number column of the statement and mark off those checks paid on your check register. Checks that are not magnetically prenumbered are listed in the order the bank pays them and will need to be checked off your register also.

Any charges appearing on this statement but not appearing in your register should be deducted from your register balance before attempting to balance your register to this statement. Likewise, any credits appearing on this statement but not appearing in your register should be added to your register balance.

BANK BALANCE
shown on this statement $ _____

ADD + DEPOSITS
made but not shown on
statement because made $ _____
or received after date of
this statement. $ _____

                          TOTAL $ _____

**SUBTRACT –
CHECKS OUTSTANDING** $ _____

BALANCE
(Should agree with your
adjusted Register Balance) $ _____

CHECKS OUTSTANDING
(Written but not shown on statement because not yet received by bank)

CHECK NUMBER	AMOUNT
TOTAL	

IN CASE OF ERROR OR QUESTION ABOUT YOUR ELECTRONIC TRANSACTION, CALL US AT 555-8965 OR WRITE TO US AT P.O. BOX 23, LAURAVILLE, LA.

⌘ **Monthly Expenses—February**

FOOD .... $ _____

HOUSING

Rent (House Payment) .... $ _____

Insurance .... $ _____

Home Repairs .... $ _____

Furniture Payments .... $ _____

Phone .... $ _____

Water .... $ _____

Gas/Oil .... $ _____

Electricity .... $ _____

Appliances .... $ _____

Other .... $ _____

TOTAL $ _____

HEALTH CARE

Doctor .... $ _____

Hospital .... $ _____

X rays, Glasses .... $ _____

Medicine .... $ _____

Insurance .... $ _____

Dentist .... $ _____

TOTAL $ _____

CLOTHING

New .... $ _____

Cleaning/Repair .... $ _____

TOTAL $ _____

TRANSPORTATION

Car Payment .... $ _____

Car Repair .... $ _____

Gas/Oil .... $ _____

License .... $ _____

Insurance .... $ _____

Bus/Cab .... $ _____

TOTAL $ _____

LIFE INSURANCE .... $ _____

MISCELLANEOUS

Haircut .... $ _____

Baby-sitter .... $ _____

Hobbies .... $ _____

Trips .... $ _____

Gifts .... $ _____

Personal Needs .... $ _____

Recreation .... $ _____

Bank/ATM Service Charges .... $ _____

Petty Cash .... $ _____

Other .... $ _____

TOTAL $ _____

SAVINGS .... $ _____

HOLIDAY CLUB .... $ _____

VACATION CLUB .... $ _____

TOTAL EXPENDITURES .... $ _____

MONTHLY TAKE-HOME PAY

Paycheck .... $ _____

Spouse .... $ _____

Other Income .... $ _____

TOTAL $ _____

Watch to see if your income is less than your expenditures. If this happens, you must make cuts somewhere. If your income is more than your expenditures, you've done a great job!

Month of March

Week No. 1

Deposit—March 4, 20__

❑ one payroll check, $465.00

❑ one check for $30.00 for doing lawn mower repairs

Request $135.00 back in cash. Put $60.00 in your savings account, $15.00 in your Holiday Club account, and $15.00 in your Vacation Club account. Use $10.00 of this for gas.

⌘ **CHECK NO. 135** | March 4, 20__

MWMIDWESTERN PHONE

PAGE 1
DATE OF BILL
02/01/—
02/28/—

P.O. BOX 1980, JULIES, LA • BUSINESS OFFICE: 555-9873

Exchange: LAURAVILLE TEL. NO. 555-9876	REF.	DATE	TIME	TOLLS	AMOUNT
	01	2/06	0247	Journay	3.75
	02	2/07	0325	Jay	3.55
Your Name	03	2/09	0123	Renee	4.68
40 Park Street	04	2/15	1256	Barb	4.75
Lauraville, LA 45637	05	2/18	0236	Portagie	3.50

LOCAL SERVICE	OTHER CHARGES	TOLLS	STATE TAX	FEDERAL TAX	PREVIOUS BAL. DUE	TOTAL BILL DUE
10.26	0.00	20.23	1.28	1.10	0.00	32.87

⌘ **CHECK NO. 136** | March 5, 20__
Write a check to Mikshi's Groceries. The total bill is $24.23.

⌘ **ATM TRANSACTION** | March 5, 20__
See ATM receipt. You owe Scott for a book.

```
03/05/--      0723AM        BE1256
8582                        $30.00

xxxxxxxxxx5896

CASH
0025699858

4587 HAROLD DR.
HAROLD, LA
```

⌘ **CHECK NO. 137** | March 5, 20__
You need new license plates on your car. Write the check to the Dept. of Motor Vehicles. The total is $22.55.

⌘ **CHECK NO. 138** | March 6, 20__

	Dr. Steen and Dr. Smithee	
	NORTH JAY MEDICAL CLINIC	
DATE	**MEDICINE**	**TOTAL**
3/6	*Antibiotics*	*$14.61*

Week No. 2

Deposit—March 9, 20__
☐ one payroll check, $465.00

Request $120.00 back in cash. Put $50.00 in your savings account, $25.00 in your Holiday Club account, and $25.00 in your Vacation Club account. Use $5.00 of this on car gasoline.

⌘ **CHECK NO. 139** | March 9, 20__

Payment No. 3	**Payment No.**	**Account No.**	**Due**	**Amount Due**
	3	251-368-9	3/15	$572.95
Date_____				
Ck. No. _____				
Amount_____	**FIRST NATIONAL BANK**			
	LAURAVILLE, LA			
	Real Estate			
KEEP THIS PART FOR YOUR RECORDS	IMPORTANT: THIS COUPON SHOULD ACCOMPANY PAYMENT.			

⌘ **CHECK NO. 140** | March 10, 20__

READ METER NOW			KEEP FOR YOUR RECORDS	Your Name
				40 Park Street
JAY COUNTY				Lauraville, LA 45637
RURAL ELECTRIC			Meter No. 1452 WE	
			Acct. No. 00-003-085	RETURN THIS COPY WITH PAYMENT

From Reading	To Reading	KWH Used	Amount Due	KWH USED 1631	METER RD. ----------------
17030	17661	1631	$ 79.65		
Mo.	**Day**	**Yr.**	**Net Bill**		
2	01	—	$ 79.65	TOTAL AMOUNT DUE	
Mo.	**Day**	**Yr.**	**Bill w/Penalty**	$ 79.65	
2	28	—	$ 98.65		

⌘ **CHECK NO. 141** | March 13, 20__
You decide to buy a new outfit for yourself. Write a check for $39.95 to Remaklus Clothing Store.

⌘ **CHECK NO. 142** | March 15, 20__
You need groceries. Write a check to Laux Grocery for $25.88.

Week No. 3

Deposit—March 18, 20__

❏ one payroll check, $465.00

Request $120.00 back in cash. Put $50.00 in your savings account. Put $25.00 in your Holiday Club account. Use $10.00 of this for car gasoline.

⌘ **DEBIT CARD TRANSACTION** | March 18, 20__
See debit receipt.

```
DATE 0318--

QUAN          DESC        AMOUNT
1             CAR WASH    $32.99

2518-95-1125-5896

TOTAL         $32.99

PETE'S CAR WASH
```

⌘ **CHECK NO. 143** | March 19, 20__

KEEP THIS STUB	SRLC	S.R. Loan Co. AUTO LOAN	Payment No. 3 DUE DATE 3/22
PAYMENT NO: 3		❖**S.R. Loan Company** MAKE CHECKS PAYABLE TO: SRLC	
AMOUNT DUE: $245.00		Return this stub with payment.	**TOTAL DUE** $245.00

⌘ **CHECK NO. 144** | March 19, 20__
The water bill is due. Write a check to County Water Works for $20.54.

⌘ **CHECK NO. 145** | March 21, 20__
You needed a haircut. Write a check to Julie's Chop Shop for $12.50.

⌘ **CHECK NO. 146** | March 22, 20__

Jay's Auto Insurance
LAURAVILLE, LA

Your Name
40 Park Street
Lauraville, LA 45637

Date	Vehicle	Year	Type	Amount Insured	Total Due Semiannual
3/23	BIADD	2000	123	$100,000	$319.00

RETURN THIS COPY WITH PAYMENT.   **TOTAL** $319.00

Week No. 4

Deposit—March 25, 20__

☐ one payroll check, $465.00

Request $100.00 back in cash. Put $50.00 in your Vacation Club account. Use $25.00 of this for car gasoline.

⌘ **CHECK NO. 147** | March 25, 20__
You decide to take a weekend trip to Madison. It costs $137.00 to stay at the President Madison Inn. Pay for it by check.

⌘ **CHECK NO. 148** | March 27, 20__
Write a check to Kate's Groceries for $32.76.

⌘ **DEBIT CARD TRANSACTION** | March 28, 20__
See debit receipt.

```
DATE 0328--

QUAN          DESC        AMOUNT
  1           KNIT TOP    $38.50

2518-95-1125-5896

TOTAL $38.50

RUTH'S KNIT SHOP
```

⌘ **CHECK NO. 149** | March 28, 20__

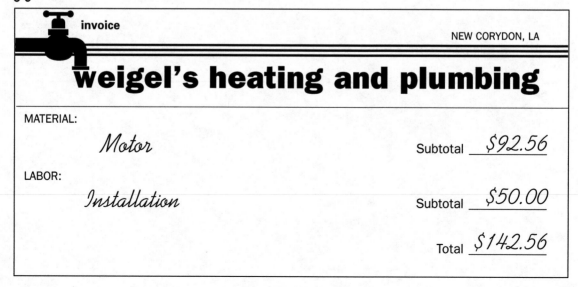

⌘ **CHECK NO. 150** | March 28, 20__
You need to buy a birthday gift for a special friend. Write a check to Loretta's Gift Shoppe for $25.16.

⌘ **ATM CARD TRANSACTION** | March 30, 20__
See ATM receipt. Your Uncle Steve paid you for helping him put on a new roof.

```
03/30/--      1111PM        BE1258
8582                        $82.50


xxxxxxxxxx5896

DEPOSIT TO CHECKING
00025688852

658 TILLY STREET
BRYANT, LA
```

⌘ **DEBIT CARD TRANSACTION** | March 30, 20__
Use your debit card to pay the following bill:

RYAN'S PRO SHOP

1 Putter	$124.00
1 Iron	$98.00
Sub total	$222.00
tax	$13.32
Total	$235.32

This is the end of the month. Follow the steps for reconciling your bank statement. Use the March bank statement, the balance sheet, the check register, and the monthly expenses form. Use the glossary for any words that you do not understand. After balancing your checkbook, continue with the next month of the simulation.

On a separate sheet, list and subtotal individual March expenditures for gas, clothing, food, trips, and so forth, as well as service charges and petty cash (cash back from paychecks and other deposits). Also keep track of other income (prizes, gifts, payment for odd jobs, and so forth).

⌘ **Activity Statement—March**

FIRST NATIONAL BANK

Lauraville, LA   March
Telephone: Your Name   Page 1
(125) 555-4562   40 Park Street
                                    Lauraville, LA 45637

                                                                Checking #251-372-8

PREVIOUS STATEMENT, NEW BALANCE OF 1179.31
5 DEPOSITS AND OTHER CREDITS TOTALING 1460.00
19 CHECKS AND OTHER DEBITS TOTALING 2048.95
SERVICE CHARGE 1.50
BALANCE AS OF 3/31/— 588.86

CHECKING ACCOUNT TRANSACTIONS...

DATE	AMOUNT	TRANSACTION DESCRIPTION
FEB. 28	45.00	ATM DEPOSIT
MAR. 4	360.00	DEPOSIT
MAR. 9	345.00	DEPOSIT
MAR. 18	345.00	DEPOSIT
MAR. 25	365.00	DEPOSIT

DATE	CK. NO.	AMOUNT	DATE	CK. NO.	AMOUNT
JAN. 25	117	52.82	MAR. 18	DEBIT	32.99
FEB. 14	126	123.95	MAR. 19	143	245.00
FEB. 27	DEBIT	23.78	MAR. 19	144	20.54
MAR. 4	135	32.87	MAR. 21	145	12.50
MAR. 5	136	24.23	MAR. 22	146	319.00
MAR. 5	ATM	30.00	MAR. 25	147	137.00
MAR. 6	137	22.55	MAR. 27	148	32.76
MAR. 9	139	572.95	MAR. 28	150	25.16
MAR. 10	140	79.65	MAR. 30	DEBIT	235.32
MAR. 15	142	25.88			

DAILY BALANCE

DATE	AMOUNT	DATE	AMOUNT
BALANCE	1179.31	MAR. 19	987.10
MAR. 1	1023.76	MAR. 21	974.60
MAR. 4	1350.89	MAR. 22	655.60
MAR. 5	1274.11	MAR. 25	883.60
MAR. 9	1046.16	MAR. 27	850.84
MAR. 10	966.51	MAR. 28	825.68
MAR. 15	940.63	MAR. 30	588.86
MAR. 18	1252.64		

⌘ **Balance Sheet—March**

This form will help you balance your bank statement.

The activity statement lists magnetically prenumbered checks in the order that you write them, not in the order the bank pays them. This saves you time as you do not need to sort checks. Simply refer to the check number column of the statement and mark off those checks paid on your check register. Checks that are not magnetically prenumbered are listed in the order the bank pays them and will need to be checked off your register also.

Any charges appearing on this statement but not appearing in your register should be deducted from your register balance before attempting to balance your register to this statement. Likewise, any credits appearing on this statement but not appearing in your register should be added to your register balance.

BANK BALANCE
shown on this statement $ _____

ADD + DEPOSITS
made but not shown on
statement because made $ _____
or received after date of
this statement. $ _____

                    TOTAL $ _____

SUBTRACT –
CHECKS OUTSTANDING $ _____

BALANCE
(Should agree with your
adjusted Register Balance) $ _____

CHECKS OUTSTANDING
(Written but not shown on statement
because not yet received by bank)

CHECK NUMBER	AMOUNT
TOTAL	

IN CASE OF ERROR OR QUESTION ABOUT YOUR ELECTRONIC TRANSACTION, CALL US AT 555-8965 OR WRITE TO US AT P.O. BOX 23, LAURAVILLE, LA.

⌘ **Monthly Expenses—March**

FOOD..................................... $ _____

HOUSING

Rent (House Payment) .... $ _____

Insurance .... $ _____

Home Repairs....................... $ _____

Furniture Payments .... $ _____

Phone................................... $ _____

Water .... $ _____

Gas/Oil .... $ _____

Electricity .... $ _____

Appliances .... $ _____

Other.................................... $ _____

TOTAL $ _____

HEALTH CARE

Doctor.................................. $ _____

Hospital................................ $ _____

X rays, Glasses .... $ _____

Medicine............................... $ _____

Insurance .... $ _____

Dentist.................................. $ _____

TOTAL $ _____

CLOTHING

New .... $ _____

Cleaning/Repair..................... $ _____

TOTAL $ _____

TRANSPORTATION

Car Payment.......................... $ _____

Car Repair .... $ _____

Gas/Oil .... $ _____

License .... $ _____

Insurance .... $ _____

Bus/Cab .... $ _____

TOTAL $ _____

LIFE INSURANCE .... $ _____

MISCELLANEOUS

Haircut .... $ _____

Baby-sitter............................ $ _____

Hobbies................................. $ _____

Trips .... $ _____

Gifts .... $ _____

Personal Needs .... $ _____

Recreation............................. $ _____

Bank/ATM Service Charges .... $ _____

Petty Cash .... $ _____

Other.................................... $ _____

TOTAL $ _____

SAVINGS .... $ _____

HOLIDAY CLUB .... $ _____

VACATION CLUB .... $ _____

TOTAL EXPENDITURES .... $ _____

MONTHLY TAKE-HOME PAY

Paycheck............................... $ _____

Spouse.................................. $ _____

Other Income .... $ _____

TOTAL $ _____

Watch to see if your income is less than your expenditures. If this happens, you must make cuts somewhere. If your income is more than your expenditures, you've done a great job!

Month of April

Week No. 1

Deposit—April 1, 20__

❏ one payroll check, $465.00

Request $225.00 back in cash. Put $100.00 in your savings account. Put $50.00 in your Holiday Club account and $50.00 in your Vacation Club account. Use $10.00 of this for gas.

⌘ **CHECK NO. 151** | April 1, 20__
You need groceries. Write a check to Wendel's Groceries for $29.85.

⌘ **CHECK NO. 152** | April 3, 20__
Write a check to Dave's Shoe Store. The total bill is $51.50.

⌘ **CHECK NO. 153** | April 6, 20__

					PAGE 1
MW MIDWESTERN PHONE					DATE OF BILL 03/01/— 03/31/—

P.O. BOX 1980, JULIES, LA • BUSINESS OFFICE 555-9873

Exchange: LAURAVILLE	REF.	DATE	TIME	TOLLS	AMOUNT
TEL. NO. 555-9876	01	03/03	0522	Portlandy	1.83
	02	03/07	0140	Jay City	2.62
Your Name	03	03/15	1231	Anderson	.83
40 Park Street	04	03/17	0806	Indie	3.98
Lauraville, LA 45637	05	03/23	0910	Alicee	4.05

LOCAL SERVICE	OTHER CHARGES	TOLLS	STATE TAX	FEDERAL TAX	PREVIOUS BAL. DUE	TOTAL BILL DUE
10.26	0.00	13.31	1.02	1.00	0.00	25.59

Week No. 2

Deposit—April 8, 20__

❏ one payroll check, $465.00

Request $320.00 back in cash. Put $100.00 in your savings account. Put $50.00 in your Holiday Club account and $50.00 in your Vacation Club account. Use $10.00 of this for cab and bus fare.

⌘ **CHECK NO. 154 |** April 8, 20__
You buy some flowers. Write a check to Ron's Flower Pot for $15.50.

⌘ **CHECK NO. 155 |** April 10, 20__
You buy some special treats for a friend. Write a check to Linda's Candy Shop for $14.56.

⌘ **CHECK NO. 156 |** April 11, 20__
You are having your mother and father over for a meal. Groceries at Theresa's Foodliner cost $37.99.

⌘ **CHECK NO. 157 |** April 12, 20__
You need a new lawn mower. Since you have some extra money in the checking account, you decide to pay the full bill. Write a check to Ron and Brett's Lawn Service for $189.72.

⌘ **DEBIT CARD TRANSACTION |** April 13, 20__
You have friends over for pizza. See debit receipt.

```
DATE 0413--

QUAN           DESC          AMOUNT
3              PIZZA         $35.50

2518-95-1125-5896

TOTAL          $35.50

CHRIS & RENAE'S QUICK PIZZA
```

Week No. 3

Deposit—April 15, 20__

❑ one payroll check, $465.00

❑ one check for $10.00 for repair work for a neighbor

Request $230.00 back in cash. Put $100.00 of this in savings. Put $50.00 in your Holiday Club account and $50.00 in your Vacation Club account. Use $5.00 of this for gas.

⌘ **CHECK NO. 158** | April 15, 20__

Payment No. 4	Payment No.	Account No.	Due	Amount Due
	4	251-368-9	4/15	$572.95
Date_____				
Ck. No. _____				
Amount_____	**FIRST NATIONAL BANK**			
	LAURAVILLE, LA			
	Real Estate			
KEEP THIS PART FOR YOUR RECORDS	IMPORTANT: THIS COUPON SHOULD ACCOMPANY PAYMENT.			

⌘ **CHECK NO. 159** | April 15, 20__
You decide to buy a raincoat. Write a check to Kevin's Coats 'n' Things for $37.31.

⌘ **CHECK NO. 160** | April 16, 20__

READ METER NOW			KEEP FOR YOUR RECORDS	Your Name 40 Park Street Lauraville, LA 45637
JAY COUNTY RURAL ELECTRIC		Meter No. 1452 WE Acct. No. 00-003-085		RETURN THIS COPY WITH PAYMENT
From Reading	**To Reading**	**KWH Used**	**Amount Due**	
17661	19261	1600	$ 75.25	KWH USED 1630 ... METER RD. ----------------
Mo.	**Day**	**Yr.**	**Net Bill**	
3	01	—	$ 75.25	
Mo.	**Day**	**Yr.**	**Bill w/Penalty**	TOTAL AMOUNT DUE
3	31	—	$ 82.26	$ 75.25

Week No. 4

Deposit—April 22, 20___

❑ one payroll check, $465.00

Request $25.00 back in cash. Use $15.00 of this cash for a haircut.

⌘ **CHECK NO. 161** | April 22, 20___

KEEP THIS STUB	**SRLC**	S.R. Loan Co.	**Payment No.** 4
		AUTO LOAN	DUE DATE 4/22
PAYMENT NO: 4		❖ **S.R. Loan Company**	
		MAKE CHECKS PAYABLE TO: SRLC	
AMOUNT DUE:		Return this stub with payment.	**TOTAL DUE**
$245.00			$245.00

⌘ **CHECK NO. 162** | April 22, 20___
The water bill is due. Write a check to County Water Works for $19.00.

⌘ **CHECK NO. 163** | April 23, 20___
You decide to buy a new chair for the living room. Payments are for six months at $50.00 a month. Make the check out to Ben's Furniture.

⌘ **ATM TRANSACTION** | April 25, 20___
Jaimie Byrd paid you $185.00 for cleaning houses. Deposit some of the money with your ATM card. See ATM receipt for amount.

```
04/25/--     1205AM      BE1258
8582                    $175.00

xxxxxxxxxx5896

DEPOSIT TO CHECKING
0002568887

568 JOSEPH ST
RYAN, AR
```

⌘ **CHECK NO. 164** | April 27, 20__
Your toaster oven broke. Pay the following bill.

JANE'S FIX-IT SHOP		
ITEM REPAIRED	PART	AMOUNT
Electrical Repairs	*Wiring*	*$7.89*

⌘ **DEBIT CARD TRANSACTION** | April 27, 20__
See debit receipt.

```
DATE 0427--

QUAN          DESC      AMOUNT
1             MONTH     $45.00

2518-95-1125-5896

              TOTAL     $45.00

WILSON'S GYM
```

This is the end of the month. Follow the steps for reconciling your bank statement. Use the April bank statement, the balance sheet, the check register, and the monthly expenses form. Use the glossary for any words that you do not understand. After balancing your checkbook, continue with the next month of the simulation.

On a separate sheet, list and subtotal individual April expenditures for gas, clothing, food, trips, and so forth, as well as service charges and petty cash (cash back from paychecks and other deposits). Also keep track of other income (prizes, gifts, payment for odd jobs, and so forth).

⌘ **Activity Statement—April**

FIRST NATIONAL BANK

Lauraville, LA
Telephone:
(125) 555-4562

Your Name
40 Park Street
Lauraville, LA 45637

April
Page 1

Checking #251-372-8

PREVIOUS STATEMENT, NEW BALANCE OF 588.86
6 DEPOSITS AND OTHER CREDITS TOTALING 1327.50
19 CHECKS AND OTHER DEBITS TOTALING 1642.84
SERVICE CHARGE 77
BALANCE AS OF 4/31— 272.75

CHECKING ACCOUNT TRANSACTIONS...

DATE	AMOUNT	TRANSACTION DESCRIPTION
MAR. 30	82.50	ATM DEPOSIT
APR. 1	240.00	DEPOSIT
APR. 8	145.00	DEPOSIT
APR. 15	245.00	DEPOSIT
APR. 22	440.00	DEPOSIT
APR. 25	175.00	ATM DEPOSIT

DATE	CK. NO.	AMOUNT	DATE	CK. NO.	AMOUNT
MAR. 6	138	14.61	APR. 12	157	189.72
MAR. 13	141	39.95	APR. 13	DEBIT	35.50
MAR. 28	149	142.56	APR. 15	158	572.95
MAR. 28	DEBIT	38.50	APR. 15	159	37.31
APR. 1	151	29.85	APR. 16	160	75.25
APR. 3	152	51.50	APR. 20		25.00OD
APR. 6	153	25.59	APR. 22	161	245.00
APR. 8	154	15.50	APR. 23	163	50.00
APR. 10	155	14.56	APR. 30	ATM CHARGE	1.50
APR. 11	156	37.99			

DAILY BALANCE

DATE	AMOUNT	DATE	AMOUNT
BALANCE	588.86	APR. 13	420.53
APR. 1	645.89	APR. 15	55.27
APR. 3	594.39	APR. 16	−19.98
APR. 6	568.80	APR. 20	−44.98
APR. 8	698.30	APR. 22	150.02
APR. 10	683.74	APR. 23	100.02
APR. 11	645.75	APR. 25	275.02
APR. 12	456.03	APR. 30	272.75

⌘ **Balance Sheet—April**

This form will help you balance your bank statement.

The activity statement lists magnetically prenumbered checks in the order that you write them, not in the order the bank pays them. This saves you time as you do not need to sort checks. Simply refer to the check number column of the statement and mark off those checks paid on your check register. Checks that are not magnetically prenumbered are listed in the order the bank pays them and will need to be checked off your register also.

Any charges appearing on this statement but not appearing in your register should be deducted from your register balance before attempting to balance your register to this statement. Likewise, any credits appearing on this statement but not appearing in your register should be added to your register balance.

BANK BALANCE
shown on this statement $ _____

ADD + DEPOSITS $ _____
made but not shown on
statement because made $ _____
or received after date of
this statement. $ _____

                        TOTAL $ _____

**SUBTRACT –
CHECKS OUTSTANDING** $ _____

BALANCE
(Should agree with your
adjusted Register Balance) $ _____

CHECKS OUTSTANDING
(Written but not shown on statement
because not yet received by bank)

CHECK NUMBER	AMOUNT
TOTAL	

IN CASE OF ERROR OR QUESTION ABOUT YOUR ELECTRONIC TRANSACTION, CALL US AT 555-8965 OR WRITE TO US AT P.O. BOX 23, LAURAVILLE, LA.

⌘ **Monthly Expenses—April**

FOOD.............................. $ _____

HOUSING

Rent (House Payment) .... $ _____

Insurance .... $ _____

Home Repairs .... $ _____

Furniture Payments .... $ _____

Phone................................. $ _____

Water .... $ _____

Gas/Oil .... $ _____

Electricity .... $ _____

Appliances .... $ _____

Other.................................. $ _____

TOTAL $ _____

HEALTH CARE

Doctor................................ $ _____

Hospital.............................. $ _____

X rays, Glasses .... $ _____

Medicine .... $ _____

Insurance .... $ _____

Dentist .... $ _____

TOTAL $ _____

CLOTHING

New .... $ _____

Cleaning/Repair.................... $ _____

TOTAL $ _____

TRANSPORTATION

Car Payment......................... $ _____

Car Repair .... $ _____

Gas/Oil .... $ _____

License .... $ _____

Insurance .... $ _____

Bus/Cab .... $ _____

TOTAL $ _____

LIFE INSURANCE .... $ _____

MISCELLANEOUS

Haircut .... $ _____

Baby-sitter........................... $ _____

Hobbies............................... $ _____

Trips .... $ _____

Gifts .... $ _____

Personal Needs .... $ _____

Recreation............................ $ _____

Bank/ATM Service Charges .... $ _____

Petty Cash .... $ _____

Other.................................. $ _____

TOTAL $ _____

SAVINGS .... $ _____

HOLIDAY CLUB .... $ _____

VACATION CLUB .... $ _____

TOTAL EXPENDITURES .... $ _____

MONTHLY TAKE-HOME PAY

Paycheck.............................. $ _____

Spouse................................. $ _____

Other Income .... $ _____

TOTAL $ _____

Watch to see if your income is less than your expenditures. If this happens, you must make cuts somewhere. If your income is more than your expenditures, you've done a great job!

Month of May

You decide to go to the bank and set up overdraft protection. This means the bank will automatically take money from your savings account to cover the checks if you overdraw your checking account. Make sure you add this deposit when balancing your account if needed.

Week No. 1

Deposit—May 1, 20__

❏ one payroll check, $465.00

❏ one check for $40.00 for an old television set you sold

❏ one check for $65.00 for winning the office pool

Request $45.00 back in cash. Use $10.00 of this to rent a boat for fishing on Blue Lake.

⌘ **CHECK NO. 165** | May 3, 20__
You need some gardening supplies. Write a check to Brian's Hardware for $69.27.

⌘ **ATM CARD TRANSACTION** | May 4, 20__
See ATM receipt. Andy paid you $75.00 for an old mirror. Deposit some of the money.

```
0504--          0945AM      BE1225
8582                        $50.00


xxxxxxxxxx5896

DEPOSIT TO CHECKING
0002568855

687 ANDREW RD
PORTLAND, LA
```

⌘ **CHECK NO. 166** | May 5, 20__
A window has broken in your house. Pay the following.

Glass House Lauraville, LA

RECEIPT

1 glass replacement	$16.05
Tax	1.25
	$17.30

Week No. 2

Deposit—May 6, 20__

❏ one payroll check, $465.00

Request $225.00 back in cash. Put $75.00 in your savings account and $100.00 in your Vacation Club account. Use $15.00 for gas.

⌘ **CHECK NO. 167** | May 7, 20__
You need a few groceries. Write a check to Laux Grocery for $18.62.

⌘ **CHECK NO. 168** | May 7, 20__

MW MIDWESTERN PHONE

P.O. BOX 1980, JULIES, LA • BUSINESS OFFICE: 555-9873

PAGE 1
DATE OF BILL
04/01/—
04/30/—

Exchange: LAURAVILLE TEL. NO. 555-9876		REF.	DATE	TIME	TOLLS	AMOUNT
		01	4/02	0233	French	2.87
		02	4/07	0147	Bryant	4.36
Your Name		03	4/16	1252	Peterville	1.82
40 Park Street		04	4/17	0408	Mary	.42
Lauraville, LA 45637		05	4/28	0542	Judy	1.99

LOCAL SERVICE	OTHER CHARGES	TOLLS	STATE TAX	FEDERAL TAX	PREVIOUS BAL. DUE	TOTAL BILL DUE
10.26	0.00	11.46	1.20	1.03	0.00	23.95

⌘ **CHECK NO. 169** | May 11, 20__
Write a check to Windmiller Drugs. The cost of the shampoo and soap was $6.79.

Week No. 3

Deposit—May 15, 20__

❏ one payroll check, $465.00

Request $120.00 back in cash. Put $100.00 of this in savings and use $5.00 of this for gas.

⌘ **CHECK NO. 170** | May 15, 20__

Payment No. 5	Payment No.	Account No.	Due	Amount Due
	5	251-368-9	5/15	$572.95

Date_____

Ck. No. _____

Amount_____

FIRST NATIONAL BANK

LAURAVILLE, LA

Real Estate

KEEP THIS PART
FOR YOUR RECORDS

IMPORTANT: THIS COUPON SHOULD ACCOMPANY PAYMENT.

⌘ **CHECK NO. 171** | May 16, 20__
Pay $25.00 for a month's dues to the Recreation Club.

⌘ **CHECK NO. 172** | May 16, 20__

READ METER NOW   KEEP FOR YOUR RECORDS

JAY COUNTY RURAL ELECTRIC

Meter No. 1452 WE
Acct. No. 00-003-085

Your Name
40 Park Street
Lauraville, LA 45637

RETURN THIS COPY WITH PAYMENT

From Reading	To Reading	KWH Used	Amount Due
19261	20643	1382	$ 63.42
Mo.	**Day**	**Yr.**	**Net Bill**
4	01	—	$ 63.42
Mo.	**Day**	**Yr.**	**Bill w/Penalty**
4	30	—	$ 68.42

KWH USED 1631

METER RD.

TOTAL AMOUNT DUE
$ 63.42

After you paid this bill, you signed an agreement with the electric company to have them automatically take money out of your account once a month to pay the electric bill. Watch for the correct amount on your next month's statement. It will be taken out the 15th of each month. It will show up as 8999 under the check number. Make sure you subtract it from your records.

⌘ **DEBIT CARD TRANSACTION** | May 19, 20__
See debit receipt.

```
DATE 0519--

QUAN          DESC          AMOUNT
              RING          $59.00

2518-95-1125-5896

TOTAL        $59.00

KATIE & BETSY'S FINE JEWELRY
```

⌘ **CHECK NO. 173** | May 20, 20__

Journay Home Insurance Lauraville, LA

Your Name
40 Park Street
Lauraville, LA 45637

Due Date	Insured	Amount Insured	Amount
5/21	2002	$100,000	$186.00
		TOTAL	**$186.00**

⌘ **ATM CARD TRANSACTION** | May 20, 20__
See ATM receipt. You needed cash.

```
0520--        0859AM        BE1258
8582                        $50.00

xxxxxxxxxx5896

CASH
000256998

569 LINN ST.
DELINA, LA
```

⌘ **CHECK NO. 174** | May 20, 20__

KEEP THIS STUB	**SRLC**	**S.R. Loan Co.** AUTO LOAN	**Payment No.** 5 DUE DATE 5/22
PAYMENT NO: 5		❖ *S.R. Loan Company* MAKE CHECKS PAYABLE TO: SRLC	
AMOUNT DUE: $245.00		Return this stub with payment.	**TOTAL DUE** $245.00

Week No. 4

Deposit—May 23, 20__

❑ one payroll check, $465.00

Request $60.00 back for car repair.

⌘ **CHECK NO. 175** | May 23, 20__
The water bill is $17.81. Write a check to the County Water Works.

⌘ **CHECK NO. 176** | May 24, 20__
Write a check to Mikshi's Groceries for $12.88.

⌘ **CHECK NO. 177** | May 26, 20__

KEEP THIS STUB	**Ben's Furniture**
Payment No: 2 DUE 5/26	DUE DATE 5/26/ __
TOTAL: $50.00	**TOTAL DUE: $50.00**

⌘ **CHECK NO. 178** | May 29, 20__

You bought a gift for your mother. Write a check for $15.99 to Loretta's Gift Shoppe.

⌘ **DEBIT CARD TRANSACTION** | May 29, 20__

Use your debit card to pay the following bill:

Jack's Beach Shop

Paddleboat rental 1 hr. $32.00

Thanks for your business!

This is the end of the month. Follow the steps for reconciling your bank statement. Use the May bank statement, the balance sheet, the check register, and the monthly expenses form. Use the glossary for any words that you do not understand. After balancing your checkbook, continue with the next month of the simulation.

On a separate sheet, list and subtotal individual May expenditures for gas, clothing, food, trips, and so forth, as well as service charges and petty cash (cash back from paychecks and other deposits). Also keep track of other income (prizes, gifts, payment for odd jobs, and so forth).

⌘ **Activity Statement—May**

FIRST NATIONAL BANK

Lauraville, LA
Telephone:
(125) 555-4562

Your Name
40 Park Street
Lauraville, LA 45637

May
Page 1

Checking #251-372-8

PREVIOUS STATEMENT, NEW BALANCE OF	272.75
5 DEPOSITS AND OTHER CREDITS TOTALING	1565.00
16 CHECKS AND OTHER DEBITS TOTALING	1424.85
SERVICE CHARGE	1.50
BALANCE AS OF 5/31/—	411.40

CHECKING ACCOUNT TRANSACTIONS

DATE	AMOUNT	TRANSACTION DESCRIPTION
MAY 1	525.00	DEPOSIT
MAY 4	50.00	ATM DEPOSIT
MAY 6	240.00	DEPOSIT
MAY 15	345.00	DEPOSIT
MAY 23	405.00	DEPOSIT

DATE	CK. NO.	AMOUNT	DATE	CK. NO.	AMOUNT
APR. 22	162	19.00	MAY 19	DEBIT	59.00
APR. 27	164	7.89	MAY 20	173	186.00
APR. 27	DEBIT	45.00	MAY 20	174	245.00
MAY 3	165	69.27	MAY 20	ATM	50.00
MAY 5	166	17.30	MAY 24	176	12.88
MAY 7	167	18.62	MAY 26	177	50.00
MAY 7	168	23.95	MAY 29	178	15.99
MAY 15	170	572.95	MAY 29	DEBIT	32.00

DAILY BALANCE

DATE	AMOUNT	DATE	AMOUNT
BALANCE	272.75	MAY 19	599.77
MAY 1	725.86	MAY 20	118.77
MAY 3	656.59	MAY 23	523.77
MAY 4	706.59	MAY 24	510.89
MAY 5	689.29	MAY 26	460.89
MAY 6	929.29	MAY 29	411.40
MAY 7	886.72		
MAY 15	658.77		

⌘ **Balance Sheet—May**

This form will help you balance your bank statement.

The activity statement lists magnetically prenumbered checks in the order that you write them, not in the order the bank pays them. This saves you time as you do not need to sort checks. Simply refer to the check number column of the statement and mark off those checks paid on your check register. Checks that are not magnetically prenumbered are listed in the order the bank pays them and will need to be checked off your register also.

Any charges appearing on this statement but not appearing in your register should be deducted from your register balance before attempting to balance your register to this statement. Likewise, any credits appearing on this statement but not appearing in your register should be added to your register balance.

BANK BALANCE
shown on this statement $ _____

ADD + DEPOSITS $ _____
made but not shown on
statement because made $ _____
or received after date of
this statement. $ _____

     TOTAL $ _____

SUBTRACT –
CHECKS OUTSTANDING $ _____

BALANCE
(Should agree with your
adjusted Register Balance) $ _____

CHECKS OUTSTANDING

(Written but not shown on statement
because not yet received by bank)

CHECK NUMBER	AMOUNT
TOTAL	

IN CASE OF ERROR OR QUESTION ABOUT YOUR ELECTRONIC TRANSACTION, CALL US AT 555-8965 OR WRITE TO US AT P.O. BOX 23, LAURAVILLE, LA.

⌘ **Monthly Expenses—May**

FOOD..................... $ _____

HOUSING

Rent (House Payment) .... $ _____

Insurance .... $ _____

Home Repairs...................... $ _____

Furniture Payments .... $ _____

Phone.................................... $ _____

Water .... $ _____

Gas/Oil .... $ _____

Electricity .... $ _____

Appliances .... $ _____

Other.................................... $ _____

TOTAL $ _____

HEALTH CARE

Doctor.................................. $ _____

Hospital................................ $ _____

X rays, Glasses .... $ _____

Medicine............................... $ _____

Insurance .... $ _____

Dentist .... $ _____

TOTAL $ _____

CLOTHING

New .... $ _____

Cleaning/Repair..................... $ _____

TOTAL $ _____

TRANSPORTATION

Car Payment......................... $ _____

Car Repair .... $ _____

Gas/Oil .... $ _____

License .... $ _____

Insurance .... $ _____

Bus/Cab .... $ _____

TOTAL $ _____

LIFE INSURANCE .... $ _____

MISCELLANEOUS

Haircut .... $ _____

Baby-sitter............................ $ _____

Hobbies................................ $ _____

Trips .... $ _____

Gifts .... $ _____

Personal Needs .... $ _____

Recreation............................. $ _____

Bank/ATM Service Charges .... $ _____

Petty Cash .... $ _____

Other.................................... $ _____

TOTAL $ _____

SAVINGS .... $ _____

HOLIDAY CLUB .... $ _____

VACATION CLUB .... $ _____

TOTAL EXPENDITURES .... $ _____

MONTHLY TAKE-HOME PAY

Paycheck............................... $ _____

Spouse................................. $ _____

Other Income .... $ _____

TOTAL $ _____

Watch to see if your income is less than your expenditures. If this happens, you must make cuts somewhere. If your income is more than your expenditures, you've done a great job!

Month of June

Week No. 1

Deposit—June 3, 20__

❏ one payroll check, $465.00

❏ one check for $15.00 for some CDs you sold

❏ five quarters

❏ seven dimes

⌘ **CHECK NO. 179** | June 5, 20__
You buy a few groceries. Write a check to Green Grocer for $25.50.

⌘ **CHECK NO. 180** | June 7, 20__

MW MIDWESTERN PHONE

PAGE 1
DATE OF BILL
05/01/—
05/31/—

P.O. BOX 1980, JULIES, LA • BUSINESS OFFICE: 555-9873

Exchange: LAURAVILLE
TEL. NO. 555-9876

Your Name
40 Park Street
Lauraville, LA 45637

REF.	DATE	TIME	TOLLS	AMOUNT
01	5/02	0456	Misty	4.28
02	5/04	0244	Dull	1.23
03	5/15	0116	Blooms	.76
04	5/16	1242	Watson	.82
05	5/28	0143	Bry	.52

LOCAL SERVICE	OTHER CHARGES	TOLLS	STATE TAX	FEDERAL TAX	PREVIOUS BAL. DUE	TOTAL BILL DUE
10.26	0.00	7.61	1.09	1.01	0.00	19.97

⌘ **CHECK NO. 181** | June 8, 20__
You need a new watch battery. It costs $7.96 at Stafford Jewelers.

Week No. 2

Deposit—June 10, 20__

❏ one payroll check, $465.00

❏ two checks for mowing lawns: $8.00, $10.50

Request $120.00 back in cash. Use $10.00 of this for car gasoline. Put $100.00 into your savings account.

✤ **CHECK NO. 182** | June 11, 20__
The porch needed painting. Write a check for the following bill.

Reed's Paint Store

INVOICE

1 Quart of Porch Paint	$4.80
Tax	.30
Total	$5.10

✤ **CHECK NO. 183** | June 12, 20__

Payment No. 6		Payment No.	Account No.	Due	Amount Due
		6	251-368-9	6/15	$572.95
Date_____					
Ck. No. _____		**FIRST NATIONAL BANK**			
Amount_____		LAURAVILLE, LA			
		Real Estate			
KEEP THIS PART FOR YOUR RECORDS		IMPORTANT: THIS COUPON SHOULD ACCOMPANY PAYMENT.			

✤ **DEBIT CARD TRANSACTION** | June 13, 20__
See debit receipt.

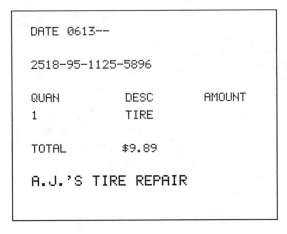

```
DATE 0613--

2518-95-1125-5896

QUAN        DESC        AMOUNT
1           TIRE

TOTAL       $9.89

A.J.'S TIRE REPAIR
```

✤ **CHECK NO. 184** | June 14, 20__
Write a check to Laux Grocery. The total cost is $18.77.

© 2006

✤ **CHECK NO. 185** | June 15, 20__
You hired Andy Hem to walk your dog. Write a check for $7.50 to him.

Week No. 3

Deposit—June 18, 20__

❑ one payroll check, $465.00

❑ one check for $35.00 for selling items on-line

❑ one check for $45.00 for fixing the neighbor's computer

Request $35.50 back in cash. Use $15.00 on gas. Spend $5.00 on personal items, such as soap and shampoo.

✤ **CHECK NO. 186** | June 19, 20__
Write a check to Alice's Sport Shop for $35.72. The sweats will come in handy at the gym.

✤ **CHECK NO. 187** | June 20, 20__

KEEP THIS STUB	**SRLC**	**S.R. Loan Co.** AUTO LOAN	**Payment No. 6** DUE DATE 6/22
PAYMENT NO: 6		**❖ S.R. Loan Company** MAKE CHECKS PAYABLE TO: SRLC	
AMOUNT DUE: $ 245.00		Return this stub with payment.	**TOTAL DUE** $245.00

✤ **ATM CARD TRANSACTION** | June 21, 20__
See ATM receipt. You won this money on a raffle ticket.

```
0621--        0724PM      BE5896
8582                      $75.00

xxxxxxxxxx5896

DEPOSIT TO CHECKING
000256899

7896 PEG ST.
COLD, LA
```

⌘ **CHECK NO. 188** | June 22, 20__
The water bill is due. Write a check to County Water Works for $23.21.

⌘ **CHECK NO. 189** | June 22, 20__
Write a check to Kari's Drugstore for $16.88. You bought personal supplies such as deodorant and aspirin.

Week No. 4

Deposit—June 24, 20__

☐ one payroll check, $465.00

Request $100.00 back in cash. Use $55.00 for gas on vacation and $30.00 for meals.

⌘ **CHECK NO. 190** | June 24, 20__
Write a check to Kristie's Cozy Inn. You will stay one night for $75.00.

⌘ **CHECK NO. 191** | June 25, 20__
You buy a souvenir. Write a check to Carrie's Unique Gifts for $32.95.

⌘ **CHECK NO. 192** | June 26, 20__
You buy some small gifts for friends and coworkers. Write a check for $28.55 to Gerri's Boutique.

⌘ **DEBIT CARD TRANSACTION** | June 28, 20__
You buy two CDs. Pay $34.87 to Lily's Record Store.

⌘ **DEBIT CARD TRANSACTION** | June 28, 20__
You decide to buy your own kayak. Use your debit card to pay the following bill:

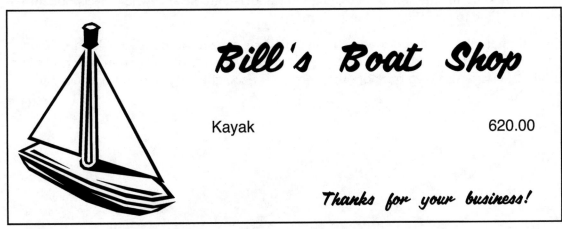

Bill's Boat Shop

Kayak   620.00

Thanks for your business!

⌘ **CHECK NO. 193** | June 29, 20__

KEEP THIS STUB	**Ben's Furniture**
Payment No: 3 DUE 6/29	DUE DATE 6/29 __
TOTAL: $50.00	**TOTAL DUE: $50.00**

Deposit—June 29, 20__

❒ one payroll check, $465.00

⌘ **ATM CARD TRANSACTION** | June 30, 20__
Barb and Tony charged you for use of their camper. Use your ATM card and pay them cash.

```
0630--          0233AM        BE5896
8582                          $50.00

xxxxxxxxxx5896

CASH
00005869985

974 KEVIN ST.
SCOTT, LA
```

This is the end of the month. Follow the steps for reconciling your bank statement. Use the June bank statement, the balance sheet, the check register, and the monthly expenses form. Use the glossary for any words that you do not understand. Balance your checkbook for the month of June to complete the simulation.

On a separate sheet, list and subtotal individual June expenditures for gas, clothing, food, trips, and so forth, as well as service charges and petty cash (cash back from paychecks and other deposits). Also keep track of other income (prizes, gifts, payment for odd jobs, and so forth).

⌘ Activity Statement—June

FIRST NATIONAL BANK

Lauraville, LA
Telephone:
(125) 555-4562

Your Name
40 Park Street
Lauraville, LA 45637

June
Page 1

Checking #251-372-8

PREVIOUS STATEMENT, NEW BALANCE OF 411.40
6 DEPOSITS AND OTHER CREDITS TOTALING 2259.95
25 CHECKS AND OTHER DEBITS TOTALING 2045.34
SERVICE CHARGE 1.25
BALANCE AS OF 6/30/— 624.76

CHECKING ACCOUNT TRANSACTIONS...

DATE	AMOUNT	TRANSACTION DESCRIPTION
JUNE 3	481.95	DEPOSIT
JUNE 10	363.50	DEPOSIT
JUNE 18	509.50	DEPOSIT
JUNE 21	75.00	ATM DEPOSIT
JUNE 24	365.00	DEPOSIT
JUNE 29	465.00	DEPOSIT

DATE	CK. NO.	AMOUNT	DATE	CK. NO.	AMOUNT
MAY 11	169	6.79	JUNE 19	186	35.72
MAY 16	171	25.00	JUNE 20	187	245.00
MAY 16	172	63.42	JUNE 22	188	23.21
MAY 23	175	17.81	JUNE 22	189	16.88
JUNE 5	179	25.50	JUNE 24	190	75.00
JUNE 7	180	19.97	JUNE 25	191	32.95
JUNE 8	181	7.96	JUNE 25	192	28.55
JUNE 11	182	5.10	JUNE 28	DEBIT	34.87
JUNE 12	183	572.95	JUNE 28	DEBIT	620.00
JUNE 13	DEBIT	9.89	JUNE 29	193	50.00
JUNE 14	184	18.77	JUNE 30	ATM	50.00
JUNE 15	185	7.50	JUNE 30	ATM CHARGE	1.50
JUNE 15	8999	51.00			

DAILY BALANCE

DATE	AMOUNT	DATE	AMOUNT
BALANCE	411.40	JUNE 15	425.19
JUNE 1	298.38	JUNE 18	934.69
JUNE 3	780.33	JUNE 19	898.97
JUNE 5	754.83	JUNE 20	653.97
JUNE 7	734.86	JUNE 21	728.97
JUNE 8	726.90	JUNE 22	688.88
JUNE 10	1090.40	JUNE 24	978.88
JUNE 11	1085.30	JUNE 25	917.38
JUNE 12	512.35	JUNE 28	262.51
JUNE 13	502.46	JUNE 29	677.51
JUNE 14	483.69	JUNE 30	624.76

⌘ **Balance Sheet—June**

This form will help you balance your bank statement.

The activity statement lists magnetically prenumbered checks in the order that you write them, not in the order the bank pays them. This saves you time as you do not need to sort checks. Simply refer to the check number column of the statement and mark off those checks paid on your check register. Checks that are not magnetically prenumbered are listed in the order the bank pays them and will need to be checked off your register also.

Any charges appearing on this statement but not appearing in your register should be deducted from your register balance before attempting to balance your register to this statement. Likewise, any credits appearing on this statement but not appearing in your register should be added to your register balance.

BANK BALANCE
shown on this statement $ _____

ADD + DEPOSITS $ _____
made but not shown on
statement because made $ _____
or received after date of
this statement. $ _____

                         TOTAL $ _____

SUBTRACT –
CHECKS OUTSTANDING $ _____

BALANCE
(Should agree with your
adjusted Register Balance) $ _____

CHECKS OUTSTANDING
(Written but not shown on statement
because not yet received by bank)

CHECK NUMBER	AMOUNT
TOTAL	

IN CASE OF ERROR OR QUESTION ABOUT YOUR ELECTRONIC TRANSACTION, CALL US AT 555-8965 OR WRITE TO US AT P.O. BOX 23, LAURAVILLE, LA.

⌘ **Monthly Expenses—June**

FOOD..................................... $ _____

HOUSING

Rent (House Payment) .... $ _____

Insurance .... $ _____

Home Repairs......................... $ _____

Furniture Payments .... $ _____

Phone .... $ _____

Water...................................... $ _____

Gas/Oil .... $ _____

Electricity .... $ _____

Appliances .... $ _____

Other .... $ _____

TOTAL $ _____

HEALTH CARE

Doctor..................................... $ _____

Hospital.................................. $ _____

X rays, Glasses .... $ _____

Medicine................................. $ _____

Insurance .... $ _____

Dentist .... $ _____

TOTAL $ _____

CLOTHING

New .... $ _____

Cleaning/Repair...................... $ _____

TOTAL $ _____

TRANSPORTATION

Car Payment........................... $ _____

Car Repair .... $ _____

Gas/Oil .... $ _____

License .... $ _____

Insurance .... $ _____

Bus/Cab .... $ _____

TOTAL $ _____

LIFE INSURANCE .... $ _____

MISCELLANEOUS

Haircut .... $ _____

Baby-sitter.............................. $ _____

Hobbies................................... $ _____

Trips .... $ _____

Gifts .... $ _____

Personal Needs .... $ _____

Recreation............................... $ _____

Bank/ATM Service Charges .... $ _____

Petty Cash .... $ _____

Other....................................... $ _____

TOTAL $ _____

SAVINGS .... $ _____

HOLIDAY CLUB .... $ _____

VACATION CLUB .... $ _____

TOTAL EXPENDITURES .... $ _____

MONTHLY TAKE-HOME PAY

Paycheck................................. $ _____

Spouse.................................... $ _____

Other Income .... $ _____

TOTAL $ _____

Watch to see if your income is less than your expenditures. If this happens, you must make cuts somewhere. If your income is more than your expenditures, you've done a great job!

⌘ **Deposit Record**

DEPOSIT RECORD

_____
PRINT NAME

_____
PRINT ADDRESS

ACCOUNT CODE NO _____

FOR YOUR CONVENIENCE, A PLACE TO RECORD AUTOMATIC PAYMENTS/DEPOSITS IS LOCATED IN BACK.

SUGGESTIONS FOR USE OF THIS REGISTER ARE PRINTED ON INSIDE FRONT COVER.

⌘ **Deposit Slips**

DEPOSIT TICKET

CASH		
LIST CHECKS SINGLY		
TOTAL FROM OTHER SIDE		
TOTAL		
LESS CASH RECEIVED		
NET DEPOSIT		

71-587/749

USE OTHER SIDE FOR
ADDITIONAL LISTING

BE SURE EACH ITEM IS
PROPERLY ENDORSED

DATE _____ 20_____

_____
ACKNOWLEDGE RECEIPT OF CASH RETURNED BY SIGNING ABOVE.

FIRST NATIONAL BANK

⑆074905872⑆   251⑈372⑈8⑈

CHECKS AND OTHER ITEMS ARE RECEIVED FOR DEPOSIT SUBJECT TO THE PROVISIONS OF THE UNIFORM COMMERCIAL CODE OR ANY APPLICABLE COLLECTION AGREEMENT.

DEPOSIT TICKET

CASH		
LIST CHECKS SINGLY		
TOTAL FROM OTHER SIDE		
TOTAL		
LESS CASH RECEIVED		
NET DEPOSIT		

71-587/749

USE OTHER SIDE FOR
ADDITIONAL LISTING

BE SURE EACH ITEM IS
PROPERLY ENDORSED

DATE _____ 20_____

_____
ACKNOWLEDGE RECEIPT OF CASH RETURNED BY SIGNING ABOVE.

FIRST NATIONAL BANK

⑆074905872⑆   251⑈372⑈8⑈

CHECKS AND OTHER ITEMS ARE RECEIVED FOR DEPOSIT SUBJECT TO THE PROVISIONS OF THE UNIFORM COMMERCIAL CODE OR ANY APPLICABLE COLLECTION AGREEMENT.

DEPOSIT TICKET

CASH		
LIST CHECKS SINGLY		
TOTAL FROM OTHER SIDE		
TOTAL		
LESS CASH RECEIVED		
NET DEPOSIT		

71-587/749

USE OTHER SIDE FOR
ADDITIONAL LISTING

BE SURE EACH ITEM IS
PROPERLY ENDORSED

DATE _____ 20_____

_____
ACKNOWLEDGE RECEIPT OF CASH RETURNED BY SIGNING ABOVE.

FIRST NATIONAL BANK

⑆074905872⑆   251⑈372⑈8⑈

CHECKS AND OTHER ITEMS ARE RECEIVED FOR DEPOSIT SUBJECT TO THE PROVISIONS OF THE UNIFORM COMMERCIAL CODE OR ANY APPLICABLE COLLECTION AGREEMENT.

⌘ **Deposit Slips**

DEPOSIT TICKET

CASH		
LIST CHECKS SINGLY		
TOTAL FROM OTHER SIDE		
TOTAL		
LESS CASH RECEIVED		
NET DEPOSIT		

71-587/749

USE OTHER SIDE FOR
ADDITIONAL LISTING

BE SURE EACH ITEM IS
PROPERLY ENDORSED

DATE _____ 20_____

_____
ACKNOWLEDGE RECEIPT OF CASH RETURNED BY SIGNING ABOVE.

FIRST NATIONAL BANK

⑈074905872⑈   251⑈372⑈8⑈

CHECKS AND OTHER ITEMS ARE RECEIVED FOR DEPOSIT SUBJECT TO THE PROVISIONS OF THE UNIFORM COMMERCIAL CODE OR ANY APPLICABLE COLLECTION AGREEMENT.

DEPOSIT TICKET

CASH		
LIST CHECKS SINGLY		
TOTAL FROM OTHER SIDE		
TOTAL		
LESS CASH RECEIVED		
NET DEPOSIT		

71-587/749

USE OTHER SIDE FOR
ADDITIONAL LISTING

BE SURE EACH ITEM IS
PROPERLY ENDORSED

DATE _____ 20_____

_____
ACKNOWLEDGE RECEIPT OF CASH RETURNED BY SIGNING ABOVE.

FIRST NATIONAL BANK

⑈074905872⑈   251⑈372⑈8⑈

CHECKS AND OTHER ITEMS ARE RECEIVED FOR DEPOSIT SUBJECT TO THE PROVISIONS OF THE UNIFORM COMMERCIAL CODE OR ANY APPLICABLE COLLECTION AGREEMENT.

DEPOSIT TICKET

CASH		
LIST CHECKS SINGLY		
TOTAL FROM OTHER SIDE		
TOTAL		
LESS CASH RECEIVED		
NET DEPOSIT		

71-587/749

USE OTHER SIDE FOR
ADDITIONAL LISTING

BE SURE EACH ITEM IS
PROPERLY ENDORSED

DATE _____ 20_____

_____
ACKNOWLEDGE RECEIPT OF CASH RETURNED BY SIGNING ABOVE.

FIRST NATIONAL BANK

⑈074905872⑈   251⑈372⑈8⑈

CHECKS AND OTHER ITEMS ARE RECEIVED FOR DEPOSIT SUBJECT TO THE PROVISIONS OF THE UNIFORM COMMERCIAL CODE OR ANY APPLICABLE COLLECTION AGREEMENT.

⌘ **Deposit Slips**

DEPOSIT TICKET

CASH		
LIST CHECKS SINGLY		
TOTAL FROM OTHER SIDE		
TOTAL		
LESS CASH RECEIVED		
NET DEPOSIT		

71-587/749

USE OTHER SIDE FOR
ADDITIONAL LISTING

BE SURE EACH ITEM IS
PROPERLY ENDORSED

DATE _____ 20 _____

_____
ACKNOWLEDGE RECEIPT OF CASH RETURNED BY SIGNING ABOVE.

FIRST NATIONAL BANK

⑈0749058720⑈   251⑈372⑈8⑈

CHECKS AND OTHER ITEMS ARE RECEIVED FOR DEPOSIT SUBJECT TO THE PROVISIONS OF THE UNIFORM COMMERCIAL CODE OR ANY APPLICABLE COLLECTION AGREEMENT.

DEPOSIT TICKET

CASH		
LIST CHECKS SINGLY		
TOTAL FROM OTHER SIDE		
TOTAL		
LESS CASH RECEIVED		
NET DEPOSIT		

71-587/749

USE OTHER SIDE FOR
ADDITIONAL LISTING

BE SURE EACH ITEM IS
PROPERLY ENDORSED

DATE _____ 20 _____

_____
ACKNOWLEDGE RECEIPT OF CASH RETURNED BY SIGNING ABOVE.

FIRST NATIONAL BANK

⑈0749058720⑈   251⑈372⑈8⑈

CHECKS AND OTHER ITEMS ARE RECEIVED FOR DEPOSIT SUBJECT TO THE PROVISIONS OF THE UNIFORM COMMERCIAL CODE OR ANY APPLICABLE COLLECTION AGREEMENT.

DEPOSIT TICKET

CASH		
LIST CHECKS SINGLY		
TOTAL FROM OTHER SIDE		
TOTAL		
LESS CASH RECEIVED		
NET DEPOSIT		

71-587/749

USE OTHER SIDE FOR
ADDITIONAL LISTING

BE SURE EACH ITEM IS
PROPERLY ENDORSED

DATE _____ 20 _____

_____
ACKNOWLEDGE RECEIPT OF CASH RETURNED BY SIGNING ABOVE.

FIRST NATIONAL BANK

⑈0749058720⑈   251⑈372⑈8⑈

CHECKS AND OTHER ITEMS ARE RECEIVED FOR DEPOSIT SUBJECT TO THE PROVISIONS OF THE UNIFORM COMMERCIAL CODE OR ANY APPLICABLE COLLECTION AGREEMENT.

⌘ Deposit Slips

DEPOSIT TICKET

CASH		
LIST CHECKS SINGLY		
TOTAL FROM OTHER SIDE		
TOTAL		
LESS CASH RECEIVED		
NET DEPOSIT		

71-587/749

USE OTHER SIDE FOR
ADDITIONAL LISTING

BE SURE EACH ITEM IS
PROPERLY ENDORSED

DATE _____ 20 _____

_____
ACKNOWLEDGE RECEIPT OF CASH RETURNED BY SIGNING ABOVE.

FIRST NATIONAL BANK

⑆0749058872⑆   251⑈372⑈8⑈

CHECKS AND OTHER ITEMS ARE RECEIVED FOR DEPOSIT SUBJECT TO THE PROVISIONS OF THE UNIFORM COMMERCIAL CODE OR ANY APPLICABLE COLLECTION AGREEMENT.

DEPOSIT TICKET

CASH		
LIST CHECKS SINGLY		
TOTAL FROM OTHER SIDE		
TOTAL		
LESS CASH RECEIVED		
NET DEPOSIT		

71-587/749

USE OTHER SIDE FOR
ADDITIONAL LISTING

BE SURE EACH ITEM IS
PROPERLY ENDORSED

DATE _____ 20 _____

_____
ACKNOWLEDGE RECEIPT OF CASH RETURNED BY SIGNING ABOVE.

FIRST NATIONAL BANK

⑆0749058872⑆   251⑈372⑈8⑈

CHECKS AND OTHER ITEMS ARE RECEIVED FOR DEPOSIT SUBJECT TO THE PROVISIONS OF THE UNIFORM COMMERCIAL CODE OR ANY APPLICABLE COLLECTION AGREEMENT.

DEPOSIT TICKET

CASH		
LIST CHECKS SINGLY		
TOTAL FROM OTHER SIDE		
TOTAL		
LESS CASH RECEIVED		
NET DEPOSIT		

71-587/749

USE OTHER SIDE FOR
ADDITIONAL LISTING

BE SURE EACH ITEM IS
PROPERLY ENDORSED

DATE _____ 20 _____

_____
ACKNOWLEDGE RECEIPT OF CASH RETURNED BY SIGNING ABOVE.

FIRST NATIONAL BANK

⑆0749058872⑆   251⑈372⑈8⑈

CHECKS AND OTHER ITEMS ARE RECEIVED FOR DEPOSIT SUBJECT TO THE PROVISIONS OF THE UNIFORM COMMERCIAL CODE OR ANY APPLICABLE COLLECTION AGREEMENT.

⌘ Deposit Slips

DEPOSIT TICKET

CASH		
LIST CHECKS SINGLY		
TOTAL FROM OTHER SIDE		
TOTAL		
LESS CASH RECEIVED		
NET DEPOSIT		

71-587/749

USE OTHER SIDE FOR
ADDITIONAL LISTING

BE SURE EACH ITEM IS
PROPERLY ENDORSED

DATE _____ 20_____

_____
ACKNOWLEDGE RECEIPT OF CASH RETURNED BY SIGNING ABOVE.

FIRST NATIONAL BANK

⑆074905872⑆   251⑈372⑈8⑈

CHECKS AND OTHER ITEMS ARE RECEIVED FOR DEPOSIT SUBJECT TO THE PROVISIONS OF THE UNIFORM COMMERCIAL CODE OR ANY APPLICABLE COLLECTION AGREEMENT.

DEPOSIT TICKET

CASH		
LIST CHECKS SINGLY		
TOTAL FROM OTHER SIDE		
TOTAL		
LESS CASH RECEIVED		
NET DEPOSIT		

71-587/749

USE OTHER SIDE FOR
ADDITIONAL LISTING

BE SURE EACH ITEM IS
PROPERLY ENDORSED

DATE _____ 20_____

_____
ACKNOWLEDGE RECEIPT OF CASH RETURNED BY SIGNING ABOVE.

FIRST NATIONAL BANK

⑆074905872⑆   251⑈372⑈8⑈

CHECKS AND OTHER ITEMS ARE RECEIVED FOR DEPOSIT SUBJECT TO THE PROVISIONS OF THE UNIFORM COMMERCIAL CODE OR ANY APPLICABLE COLLECTION AGREEMENT.

DEPOSIT TICKET

CASH		
LIST CHECKS SINGLY		
TOTAL FROM OTHER SIDE		
TOTAL		
LESS CASH RECEIVED		
NET DEPOSIT		

71-587/749

USE OTHER SIDE FOR
ADDITIONAL LISTING

BE SURE EACH ITEM IS
PROPERLY ENDORSED

DATE _____ 20_____

_____
ACKNOWLEDGE RECEIPT OF CASH RETURNED BY SIGNING ABOVE.

FIRST NATIONAL BANK

⑆074905872⑆   251⑈372⑈8⑈

CHECKS AND OTHER ITEMS ARE RECEIVED FOR DEPOSIT SUBJECT TO THE PROVISIONS OF THE UNIFORM COMMERCIAL CODE OR ANY APPLICABLE COLLECTION AGREEMENT.

⌘ Deposit Slips

DEPOSIT TICKET

CASH		
LIST CHECKS SINGLY		
TOTAL FROM OTHER SIDE		
TOTAL		
LESS CASH RECEIVED		
NET DEPOSIT		

71-587/749

USE OTHER SIDE FOR ADDITIONAL LISTING

BE SURE EACH ITEM IS PROPERLY ENDORSED

DATE _____ 20_____

_____
ACKNOWLEDGE RECEIPT OF CASH RETURNED BY SIGNING ABOVE.

FIRST NATIONAL BANK

⑆074905872⑆ 251⑈372⑈8⑉

CHECKS AND OTHER ITEMS ARE RECEIVED FOR DEPOSIT SUBJECT TO THE PROVISIONS OF THE UNIFORM COMMERCIAL CODE OR ANY APPLICABLE COLLECTION AGREEMENT.

DEPOSIT TICKET

CASH		
LIST CHECKS SINGLY		
TOTAL FROM OTHER SIDE		
TOTAL		
LESS CASH RECEIVED		
NET DEPOSIT		

71-587/749

USE OTHER SIDE FOR ADDITIONAL LISTING

BE SURE EACH ITEM IS PROPERLY ENDORSED

DATE _____ 20_____

_____
ACKNOWLEDGE RECEIPT OF CASH RETURNED BY SIGNING ABOVE.

FIRST NATIONAL BANK

⑆074905872⑆ 251⑈372⑈8⑉

CHECKS AND OTHER ITEMS ARE RECEIVED FOR DEPOSIT SUBJECT TO THE PROVISIONS OF THE UNIFORM COMMERCIAL CODE OR ANY APPLICABLE COLLECTION AGREEMENT.

DEPOSIT TICKET

CASH		
LIST CHECKS SINGLY		
TOTAL FROM OTHER SIDE		
TOTAL		
LESS CASH RECEIVED		
NET DEPOSIT		

71-587/749

USE OTHER SIDE FOR ADDITIONAL LISTING

BE SURE EACH ITEM IS PROPERLY ENDORSED

DATE _____ 20_____

_____
ACKNOWLEDGE RECEIPT OF CASH RETURNED BY SIGNING ABOVE.

FIRST NATIONAL BANK

⑆074905872⑆ 251⑈372⑈8⑉

CHECKS AND OTHER ITEMS ARE RECEIVED FOR DEPOSIT SUBJECT TO THE PROVISIONS OF THE UNIFORM COMMERCIAL CODE OR ANY APPLICABLE COLLECTION AGREEMENT.

⌘ Deposit Slips

DEPOSIT TICKET

CASH		
LIST CHECKS SINGLY		
TOTAL FROM OTHER SIDE		
TOTAL		
LESS CASH RECEIVED		
NET DEPOSIT		

71-587/749

USE OTHER SIDE FOR
ADDITIONAL LISTING

BE SURE EACH ITEM IS
PROPERLY ENDORSED

DATE _____ 20 _____

_____
ACKNOWLEDGE RECEIPT OF CASH RETURNED BY SIGNING ABOVE.

FIRST NATIONAL BANK

⑈074905872⑈ 251⑈372⑈8⑈

CHECKS AND OTHER ITEMS ARE RECEIVED FOR DEPOSIT SUBJECT TO THE PROVISIONS OF THE UNIFORM COMMERCIAL CODE OR ANY APPLICABLE COLLECTION AGREEMENT.

DEPOSIT TICKET

CASH		
LIST CHECKS SINGLY		
TOTAL FROM OTHER SIDE		
TOTAL		
LESS CASH RECEIVED		
NET DEPOSIT		

71-587/749

USE OTHER SIDE FOR
ADDITIONAL LISTING

BE SURE EACH ITEM IS
PROPERLY ENDORSED

DATE _____ 20 _____

_____
ACKNOWLEDGE RECEIPT OF CASH RETURNED BY SIGNING ABOVE.

FIRST NATIONAL BANK

⑈074905872⑈ 251⑈372⑈8⑈

CHECKS AND OTHER ITEMS ARE RECEIVED FOR DEPOSIT SUBJECT TO THE PROVISIONS OF THE UNIFORM COMMERCIAL CODE OR ANY APPLICABLE COLLECTION AGREEMENT.

DEPOSIT TICKET

CASH		
LIST CHECKS SINGLY		
TOTAL FROM OTHER SIDE		
TOTAL		
LESS CASH RECEIVED		
NET DEPOSIT		

71-587/749

USE OTHER SIDE FOR
ADDITIONAL LISTING

BE SURE EACH ITEM IS
PROPERLY ENDORSED

DATE _____ 20 _____

_____
ACKNOWLEDGE RECEIPT OF CASH RETURNED BY SIGNING ABOVE.

FIRST NATIONAL BANK

⑈074905872⑈ 251⑈372⑈8⑈

CHECKS AND OTHER ITEMS ARE RECEIVED FOR DEPOSIT SUBJECT TO THE PROVISIONS OF THE UNIFORM COMMERCIAL CODE OR ANY APPLICABLE COLLECTION AGREEMENT.

⌘ Deposit Slips

DEPOSIT TICKET

CASH		
LIST CHECKS SINGLY		
TOTAL FROM OTHER SIDE		
TOTAL		
LESS CASH RECEIVED		
NET DEPOSIT		

71-587/749

USE OTHER SIDE FOR
ADDITIONAL LISTING

BE SURE EACH ITEM IS
PROPERLY ENDORSED

DATE _____ 20 _____

_____
ACKNOWLEDGE RECEIPT OF CASH RETURNED BY SIGNING ABOVE.

FIRST NATIONAL BANK

⑆074905872⑆ 251⑈372⑈8⑇

CHECKS AND OTHER ITEMS ARE RECEIVED FOR DEPOSIT SUBJECT TO THE PROVISIONS OF THE UNIFORM COMMERCIAL CODE OR ANY APPLICABLE COLLECTION AGREEMENT.

DEPOSIT TICKET

CASH		
LIST CHECKS SINGLY		
TOTAL FROM OTHER SIDE		
TOTAL		
LESS CASH RECEIVED		
NET DEPOSIT		

71-587/749

USE OTHER SIDE FOR
ADDITIONAL LISTING

BE SURE EACH ITEM IS
PROPERLY ENDORSED

DATE _____ 20 _____

_____
ACKNOWLEDGE RECEIPT OF CASH RETURNED BY SIGNING ABOVE.

FIRST NATIONAL BANK

⑆074905872⑆ 251⑈372⑈8⑇

CHECKS AND OTHER ITEMS ARE RECEIVED FOR DEPOSIT SUBJECT TO THE PROVISIONS OF THE UNIFORM COMMERCIAL CODE OR ANY APPLICABLE COLLECTION AGREEMENT.

DEPOSIT TICKET

CASH		
LIST CHECKS SINGLY		
TOTAL FROM OTHER SIDE		
TOTAL		
LESS CASH RECEIVED		
NET DEPOSIT		

71-587/749

USE OTHER SIDE FOR
ADDITIONAL LISTING

BE SURE EACH ITEM IS
PROPERLY ENDORSED

DATE _____ 20 _____

_____
ACKNOWLEDGE RECEIPT OF CASH RETURNED BY SIGNING ABOVE.

FIRST NATIONAL BANK

⑆074905872⑆ 251⑈372⑈8⑇

CHECKS AND OTHER ITEMS ARE RECEIVED FOR DEPOSIT SUBJECT TO THE PROVISIONS OF THE UNIFORM COMMERCIAL CODE OR ANY APPLICABLE COLLECTION AGREEMENT.

⌘ **Deposit Slips**

DEPOSIT TICKET

CASH		
LIST CHECKS SINGLY		
TOTAL FROM OTHER SIDE		
TOTAL		
LESS CASH RECEIVED		
NET DEPOSIT		

71-587/749

USE OTHER SIDE FOR
ADDITIONAL LISTING

BE SURE EACH ITEM IS
PROPERLY ENDORSED

DATE _____ 20_____

_____
ACKNOWLEDGE RECEIPT OF CASH RETURNED BY SIGNING ABOVE.

FIRST NATIONAL BANK

⑈0749058721⑈   251⑊372⑊8⑈

CHECKS AND OTHER ITEMS ARE RECEIVED FOR DEPOSIT SUBJECT TO THE PROVISIONS OF THE UNIFORM COMMERCIAL CODE OR ANY APPLICABLE COLLECTION AGREEMENT.

DEPOSIT TICKET

CASH		
LIST CHECKS SINGLY		
TOTAL FROM OTHER SIDE		
TOTAL		
LESS CASH RECEIVED		
NET DEPOSIT		

71-587/749

USE OTHER SIDE FOR
ADDITIONAL LISTING

BE SURE EACH ITEM IS
PROPERLY ENDORSED

DATE _____ 20_____

_____
ACKNOWLEDGE RECEIPT OF CASH RETURNED BY SIGNING ABOVE.

FIRST NATIONAL BANK

⑈0749058721⑈   251⑊372⑊8⑈

CHECKS AND OTHER ITEMS ARE RECEIVED FOR DEPOSIT SUBJECT TO THE PROVISIONS OF THE UNIFORM COMMERCIAL CODE OR ANY APPLICABLE COLLECTION AGREEMENT.

DEPOSIT TICKET

CASH		
LIST CHECKS SINGLY		
TOTAL FROM OTHER SIDE		
TOTAL		
LESS CASH RECEIVED		
NET DEPOSIT		

71-587/749

USE OTHER SIDE FOR
ADDITIONAL LISTING

BE SURE EACH ITEM IS
PROPERLY ENDORSED

DATE _____ 20_____

_____
ACKNOWLEDGE RECEIPT OF CASH RETURNED BY SIGNING ABOVE.

FIRST NATIONAL BANK

⑈0749058721⑈   251⑊372⑊8⑈

CHECKS AND OTHER ITEMS ARE RECEIVED FOR DEPOSIT SUBJECT TO THE PROVISIONS OF THE UNIFORM COMMERCIAL CODE OR ANY APPLICABLE COLLECTION AGREEMENT.

© 2006

⌘ **Deposit Slips**

DEPOSIT TICKET

CASH		
LIST CHECKS SINGLY		
TOTAL FROM OTHER SIDE		
TOTAL		
LESS CASH RECEIVED		
NET DEPOSIT		

71-587/749

USE OTHER SIDE FOR ADDITIONAL LISTING

BE SURE EACH ITEM IS PROPERLY ENDORSED

DATE _____ 20_____

ACKNOWLEDGE RECEIPT OF CASH RETURNED BY SIGNING ABOVE.

FIRST NATIONAL BANK

⑆074905872⑆ 251⑈372⑈8⑈

CHECKS AND OTHER ITEMS ARE RECEIVED FOR DEPOSIT SUBJECT TO THE PROVISIONS OF THE UNIFORM COMMERCIAL CODE OR ANY APPLICABLE COLLECTION AGREEMENT.

DEPOSIT TICKET

CASH		
LIST CHECKS SINGLY		
TOTAL FROM OTHER SIDE		
TOTAL		
LESS CASH RECEIVED		
NET DEPOSIT		

71-587/749

USE OTHER SIDE FOR ADDITIONAL LISTING

BE SURE EACH ITEM IS PROPERLY ENDORSED

DATE _____ 20_____

ACKNOWLEDGE RECEIPT OF CASH RETURNED BY SIGNING ABOVE.

FIRST NATIONAL BANK

⑆074905872⑆ 251⑈372⑈8⑈

CHECKS AND OTHER ITEMS ARE RECEIVED FOR DEPOSIT SUBJECT TO THE PROVISIONS OF THE UNIFORM COMMERCIAL CODE OR ANY APPLICABLE COLLECTION AGREEMENT.

DEPOSIT TICKET

CASH		
LIST CHECKS SINGLY		
TOTAL FROM OTHER SIDE		
TOTAL		
LESS CASH RECEIVED		
NET DEPOSIT		

71-587/749

USE OTHER SIDE FOR ADDITIONAL LISTING

BE SURE EACH ITEM IS PROPERLY ENDORSED

DATE _____ 20_____

ACKNOWLEDGE RECEIPT OF CASH RETURNED BY SIGNING ABOVE.

FIRST NATIONAL BANK

⑆074905872⑆ 251⑈372⑈8⑈

CHECKS AND OTHER ITEMS ARE RECEIVED FOR DEPOSIT SUBJECT TO THE PROVISIONS OF THE UNIFORM COMMERCIAL CODE OR ANY APPLICABLE COLLECTION AGREEMENT.

⌘ Check Register Page

		RECORD ALL CHARGES OR CREDITS THAT AFFECT YOUR ACCOUNT					
NUMBER	DATE	DESCRIPTION OF TRANSACTION	PAYMENT/DEBIT (−)	√T	FEE (IF ANY)	DEPOSIT/CREDIT (+)	BALANCE $

© 2006

⌘ **Check Register Page**

RECORD ALL CHARGES OR CREDITS THAT AFFECT YOUR ACCOUNT

NUMBER	DATE	DESCRIPTION OF TRANSACTION	PAYMENT/DEBIT (–)	√ T	FEE (IF ANY)	DEPOSIT/CREDIT (+)	BALANCE $	

⌘ Check Register Page

RECORD ALL CHARGES OR CREDITS THAT AFFECT YOUR ACCOUNT							
NUMBER	DATE	DESCRIPTION OF TRANSACTION	PAYMENT/DEBIT (−)	√T	FEE (IF ANY)	DEPOSIT/CREDIT (+)	BALANCE $

⌘ **Check Register Page**

RECORD ALL CHARGES OR CREDITS THAT AFFECT YOUR ACCOUNT

NUMBER	DATE	DESCRIPTION OF TRANSACTION	PAYMENT/DEBIT (−)	√ T	FEE (IF ANY)	DEPOSIT/CREDIT (+)	BALANCE $	

⌘ **Check Register Page**

		RECORD ALL CHARGES OR CREDITS THAT AFFECT YOUR ACCOUNT						
NUMBER	DATE	DESCRIPTION OF TRANSACTION	PAYMENT/DEBIT (−)	√ T	FEE (IF ANY)	DEPOSIT/CREDIT (+)	$	BALANCE

⌘ **Check Register Page**

RECORD ALL CHARGES OR CREDITS THAT AFFECT YOUR ACCOUNT

NUMBER	DATE	DESCRIPTION OF TRANSACTION	PAYMENT/DEBIT (−)		√ T	FEE (IF ANY)	DEPOSIT/CREDIT (+)	BALANCE	
								$	

⌘ **Blank Checks**

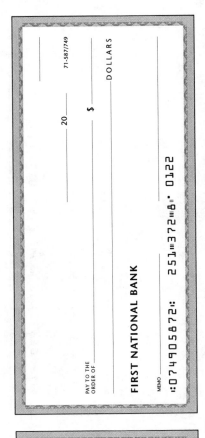

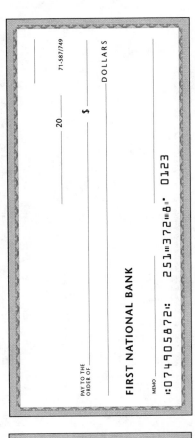

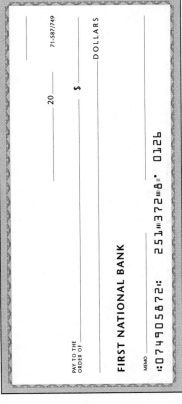

❁ **Blank Checks**

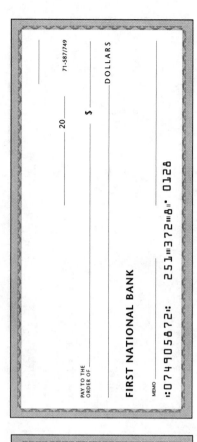

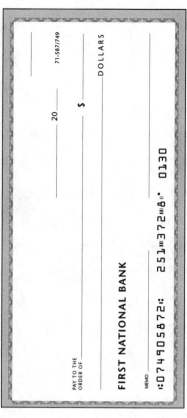

FIRST NATIONAL BANK

PAY TO THE
ORDER OF

DOLLARS

20

$

71-587/749

MEMO

⑆074905872⑆ 251⑈372⑈8⑆ 0128

FIRST NATIONAL BANK

PAY TO THE
ORDER OF

DOLLARS

20

$

71-587/749

MEMO

⑆074905872⑆ 251⑈372⑈8⑆ 0129

FIRST NATIONAL BANK

PAY TO THE
ORDER OF

DOLLARS

20

$

71-587/749

MEMO

⑆074905872⑆ 251⑈372⑈8⑆ 0130

FIRST NATIONAL BANK

PAY TO THE
ORDER OF

DOLLARS

20

$

71-587/749

MEMO

⑆074905872⑆ 251⑈372⑈8⑆ 0131

FIRST NATIONAL BANK

PAY TO THE
ORDER OF

DOLLARS

20

$

71-587/749

MEMO

⑆074905872⑆ 251⑈372⑈8⑆ 0132

FIRST NATIONAL BANK

PAY TO THE
ORDER OF

DOLLARS

20

$

71-587/749

MEMO

⑆074905872⑆ 251⑈372⑈8⑆ 0133

⌘ **Blank Checks**

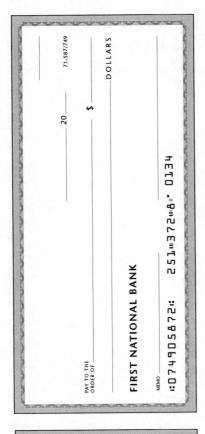

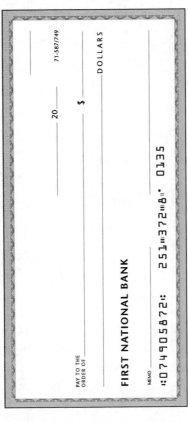

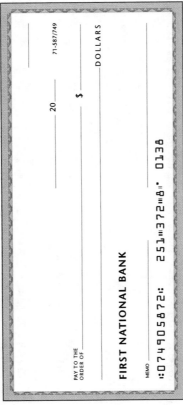

⌘ **Blank Checks**

PAY TO THE
ORDER OF

FIRST NATIONAL BANK

MEMO

20

$

DOLLARS

71-587/749

⑆074905872⑈ 251⑈372⑇8⑈⑆ 0140

PAY TO THE
ORDER OF

FIRST NATIONAL BANK

MEMO

20

$

DOLLARS

71-587/749

⑆074905872⑈ 251⑈372⑇8⑈⑆ 0141

PAY TO THE
ORDER OF

FIRST NATIONAL BANK

MEMO

20

$

DOLLARS

71-587/749

⑆074905872⑈ 251⑈372⑇8⑈⑆ 0142

PAY TO THE
ORDER OF

FIRST NATIONAL BANK

MEMO

20

$

DOLLARS

71-587/749

⑆074905872⑈ 251⑈372⑇8⑈⑆ 0143

PAY TO THE
ORDER OF

FIRST NATIONAL BANK

MEMO

20

$

DOLLARS

71-587/749

⑆074905872⑈ 251⑈372⑇8⑈⑆ 0144

PAY TO THE
ORDER OF

FIRST NATIONAL BANK

MEMO

20

$

DOLLARS

71-587/749

⑆074905872⑈ 251⑈372⑇8⑈⑆ 0145

⌘ **Blank Checks**

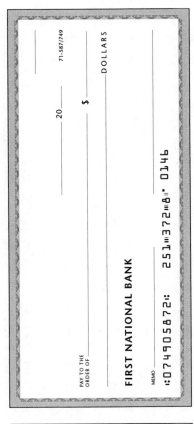

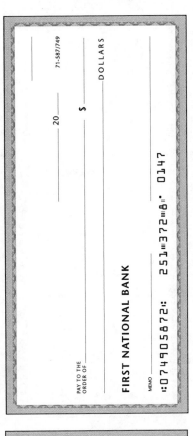

⌘ **Blank Checks**

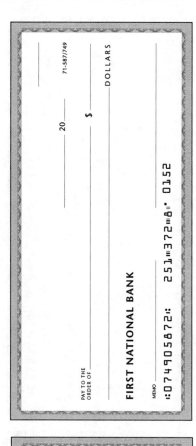

FIRST NATIONAL BANK

PAY TO THE ORDER OF

MEMO

71-587/749

20

$

DOLLARS

⑈074905872⑈ 251⑈372⑈8⑈ 0152

FIRST NATIONAL BANK

71-587/749

20

$

DOLLARS

⑈074905872⑈ 251⑈372⑈8⑈ 0153

FIRST NATIONAL BANK

71-587/749

20

$

DOLLARS

⑈074905872⑈ 251⑈372⑈8⑈ 0154

FIRST NATIONAL BANK

71-587/749

20

$

DOLLARS

⑈074905872⑈ 251⑈372⑈8⑈ 0155

FIRST NATIONAL BANK

71-587/749

20

$

DOLLARS

⑈074905872⑈ 251⑈372⑈8⑈ 0156

FIRST NATIONAL BANK

71-587/749

20

$

DOLLARS

⑈074905872⑈ 251⑈372⑈8⑈ 0157

⌘ **Blank Checks**

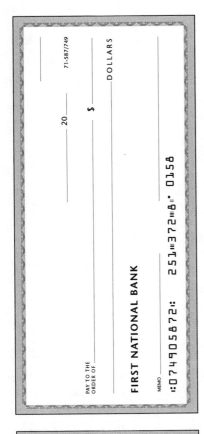

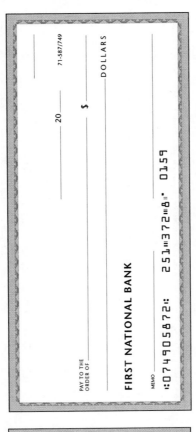

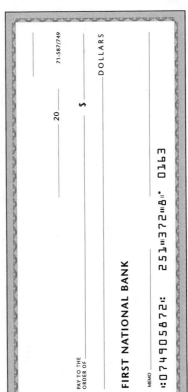

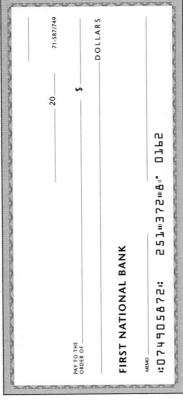

⌘ **Blank Checks**

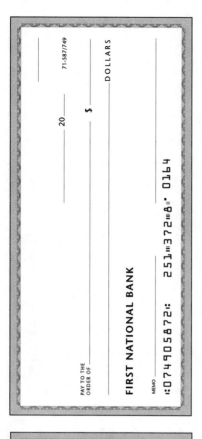

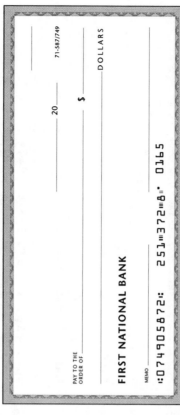

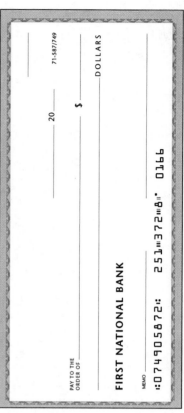

✿ **Blank Checks**

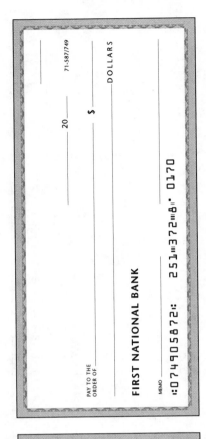

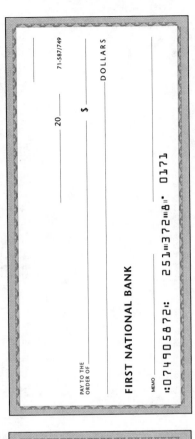

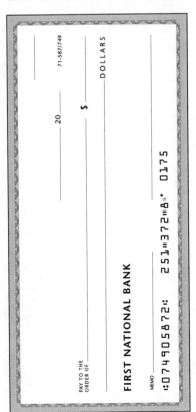

© 2006

⌘ **Blank Checks**

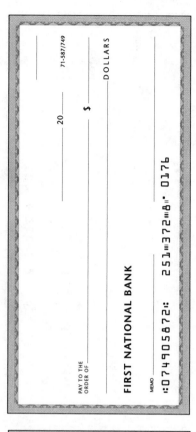

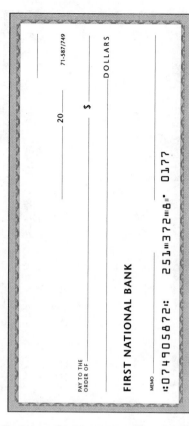

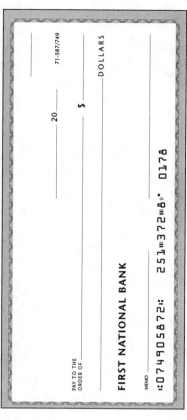

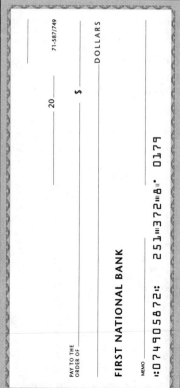

⌘ Blank Checks

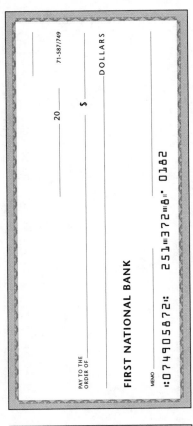

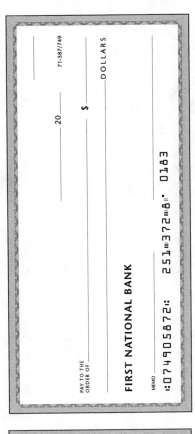

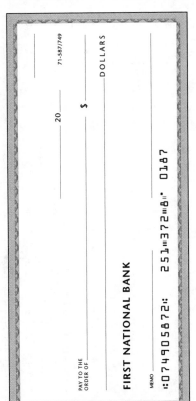

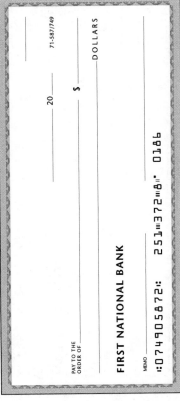

⌘ **Blank Checks**

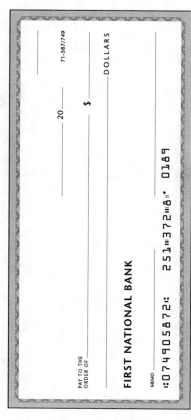

FIRST NATIONAL BANK

PAY TO THE
ORDER OF

20

$

DOLLARS

71-587/749

MEMO

⑈074905872⑈ 251⑈372⑈8⑈• 0188

FIRST NATIONAL BANK

PAY TO THE
ORDER OF

20

$

DOLLARS

71-587/749

MEMO

⑈074905872⑈ 251⑈372⑈8⑈• 0189

FIRST NATIONAL BANK

PAY TO THE
ORDER OF

20

$

DOLLARS

71-587/749

MEMO

⑈074905872⑈ 251⑈372⑈8⑈• 0190

FIRST NATIONAL BANK

PAY TO THE
ORDER OF

20

$

DOLLARS

71-587/749

MEMO

⑈074905872⑈ 251⑈372⑈8⑈• 0191

FIRST NATIONAL BANK

PAY TO THE
ORDER OF

20

$

DOLLARS

71-587/749

MEMO

⑈074905872⑈ 251⑈372⑈8⑈• 0192

FIRST NATIONAL BANK

PAY TO THE
ORDER OF

20

$

DOLLARS

71-587/749

MEMO

⑈074905872⑈ 251⑈372⑈8⑈• 0193

⌘ Blank Checks

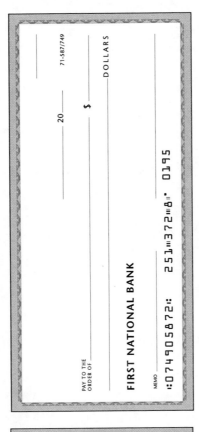